COOL GIRLS QUILT

Cool Girls Quilt

More than 15 Fresh, Fun, and Funky Projects

Linda Lum DeBono

Martingale®
& COMPANY

Cool Girls Quilt: More than 15 Fresh, Fun,
and Funky Projects
© 2007 by Linda Lum DeBono

That Patchwork Place® is an imprint
of Martingale & Company®.

Martingale & Company
20205 144th Ave. NE
Woodinville, WA 98072-8478 USA
www.martingale-pub.com

Printed in China
12 11 10 09 08 07   8 7 6 5 4 3 2 1

Library of Congress Cataloging-in-Publication Data
Library of Congress Control Number: 2007024452

ISBN: 978-1-56477-747-8

CREDITS

President & CEO: Tom Wierzbicki
Publisher: Jane Hamada
Editorial Director: Mary V. Green
Managing Editor: Tina Cook
Developmental Editor: Karen Costello Soltys
Technical Editor: Nancy Mahoney
Copy Editor: Sheila Chapman Ryan
Design Director: Stan Green
Assistant Design Director: Regina Girard
Illustrator: Adrienne Smitke
Cover Designer: Stan Green
Text Designers: Shelly Garrison & Stan Green
Photographer: Brent Kane

MISSION STATEMENT

Dedicated to providing quality products
and service to inspire creativity.

DEDICATION

To my parents, for teaching me that anything is possible

ACKNOWLEDGMENTS

Thanks to the following for inspiration along this journey.

First and foremost, to my family: Reno, for being rock solid while I've worked maniacally at my designs, and my kids, Adam and Alex, for being an inspiration. Love you the mostest!

Sally Davis and Lois Griffin: for your generosity and for being the catalyst to this whole crazy ride.

Karen Soltys: for remembering that serendipitous meeting at a Pennsylvania quilt shop and for offering me a fantastic opportunity to work with a group of passionate and wonderful people.

Mary Green, Dawn Anderson, Tina Cook, Nancy Mahoney, and Sheila Ryan: for being wonderful to work with.

Karen Junquet, Robert Fortunoff, Scott Fortunoff, Ira Schantz, Larry Reichenberg, and all of the fabulous people at Henry Glass and Company: for giving me a fantastic opportunity to design fabrics and for believing in me. I appreciate all that you do.

Heidi Kaisand, Elizabeth Tisinger, Jill Mead, and Deborah Ohrn of *American Patchwork and Quilting:* for being an awesome group of women who believe in all that I have to offer.

Nancy Weber and Jennie Brockman at Checker Distributors: I appreciate the encouragement and your belief in me right from the beginning.

Toby Preston, Linda Wood, Mary Lowe, and everyone at Kindred Quilts: you're a great bunch of gals! I am blessed.

Jan Crane and the staff at Pennington Quilt Works: thanks!

Mark Lipinski of *Quilter's Home* magazine, and Vivian Ritter of *Quilter's Newsletter Magazine:* thanks for the opportunities that you have afforded me. Great mags.

Nancy Smith, Lynda Milligan, Roseann Kermes, Amy Butler, Robyn Pandolph, Lynette Jensen, Kaye England, Jo Morten, Jackie Robinson, Cynthia Tomaszewski, Lila Scott, Alma Allen, Barb Adams, and Diane Zachowski: thanks for your inspiration, passion, and generosity.

Special thanks to the following companies who generously provided great products: Henry Glass and Company, Westminster Fibers, FreeSpirit Fabric, the Warm Company for providing Steam-a-Seam 2, Kindred Quilts, Pennington Quilt Works, and Weeks Dye Works for providing their fantastic felted wool.

Contents

introduction

This collection of designs evolved from my need to balance my design business and my family life while maintaining a level of funkiness in my products. I'm inspired by everything that surrounds me. This includes fashion, home decorating, graphic design, advertising, and crafts such as knitting and scrapbooking. I love all sorts of colors, patterns, and textures, and enjoy hip, simple projects that I can make in a jiffy. Look around and you will see that even the simplest thing—like a leaf—can inspire you and set a mood for a design.

The designs in this book are easily achievable even for the beginning quilter who has a good knowledge of sewing and basic machine-appliqué skills. My design philosophy is to keep the design elements simple and let the fabric add all of the texture, color, and sophistication to the end product. My fabric choices add extra pizzazz to each design. I know that you will be inspired to add your own personal touch with these clever projects.

The book is divided into different sections. In "Fabric" (page 11), I will give you insight into how I choose fabrics to make my projects look fresh and funky. "Quiltmaking Basics" (page 12) teaches you the basic skills to make the projects.

The first group of designs (starting on page 18) contains quick and easy projects that you can use in your crafty life. Most of the projects can be made in a day and are perfect for fast and fun gift giving. You can stitch up the adorable "Daisies in the Sky Pennants" (page 50) to perk up your design area, or carry your projects in the sophisticated "Diamonds Are a Girl's Best Bag" (page 42).

The final section (starting on page 67) includes wall hangings that you can make to brighten up your living space. The projects are spunky and make beautiful use of the contemporary fabrics that are available today.

I designed these projects for those of you who want to make fabulous yet quick and easy gifts for yourself and others. Your friends will swoon over your cool craftiness! I know that you will enjoy making this collection of projects as much as I enjoyed designing them.

All the best and enjoy!

∽ Linda

fabric

Choosing fabric can seem daunting, but it's not hard if you think it through. For me, fabric selection is driven by gut instinct, but I'll offer a few essential tips for you here.

I use 100%-cotton quilting fabric for most of my projects. When I want to add an aura of luxury, I delve into my fantastic stash of hand-printed cotton, silk, wool, and velvet.

Purpose and Mood

To select fabric, first consider the recipient of the finished project. Ask yourself questions like: Does the person have a modern and contemporary flair or traditional taste in things? Is the person an adult or child? What sort of colors does the recipient like? What sort of style do you want to express through the fabric? For example, do you want a vintage, retro, or bright-and-juvenile look?

Answering these questions will start you in the right direction, but don't be afraid to step outside the box and explore the full range of fabric styles available. We're fortunate today to have a tremendous array of fabric choices.

Organizing Your Fabrics

Before beginning a project, I start by gathering together any fabrics that have a similar visual texture (the pattern printed on the fabric) or evoke a similar feeling, regardless of the scale of the print. One pile may consist of vintage but perky fabrics whereas the next stack of fabrics may consist of bold polka dots, swirls, and stripes.

After I've arranged the fabrics according to visual texture, I regroup them into color piles, such as green, pink, blue, and so on. Arranging your fabrics in this manner before you begin a project can help you quickly see which colors you can use in your quilt. You'll have a pile of similar fabrics in both texture and color at your fingertips. This method works especially well in busy quilts such as "Love" (page 67) and "Crazy for You" (page 78), where many different textures and colors are used in one quilt.

Don't be afraid to mix and match different scales of fabrics. This gives the design contrast and places for your eyes to explore. I used prints in various scales in the "Cover Me Pretty Book Cover" (page 58). If you're going to use dramatic differences in scale, try to use fabrics from similar color groups; I find that this helps tie the project together. In this case, I used the chocolate and chartreuse group.

Another way to get all of these colors to work together is to layer. Layering with different contrasting colors and textures allows the fabrics to pop. This results in an exciting and dynamic design. You can best see an example of layering in the "Love" quilt.

Occasionally adding something unexpected can be dramatic. For example, using a black-and-white print for the binding on a bright quilt such as "Crazy for You" makes a bold statement and also ties all the bright colors together.

quiltmaking basics

THIS SECTION will serve as a quick overview of the basic skills needed to make the projects and quilts in this book. For more guidance on any of the following techniques, refer to *The Quilter's Quick Reference Guide* by Candace Eisner Strick (Martingale & Company, 2004).

Tools

You'll need a few basic supplies to make the projects in this book.

Rotary-Cutting Equipment. If you don't already own these tools, start with an 18" x 24" mat, a 45-mm rotary cutter, and a 6" x 24" ruler. The rotary cutter makes cutting fast and easy. If you are cutting large blocks, use the largest ruler you can—it makes cutting blocks much easier.

Reducing Glass. A reducing glass looks like a magnifying glass but works in the opposite way. It makes objects that are close appear as though they're far away. As I'm making color choices, I hold a reducing glass up to a group of fabrics or to an in-process project to look for areas of too much or too little contrast, something that can be hard to see when I'm standing right next to a pile of fabrics. A reducing glass is one of my essential tools—but many quilters don't use one at all. If you are hesitant about your fabric choices, try using one.

Sewing Machine. You can make all of these projects with a good but fairly basic machine. The most important features needed on the machine are a zigzag stitch for machine appliqué and the ability to lower the feed dogs for free-motion quilting. I recommend a walking foot and a free-motion foot for quilting and an embroidery foot for machine appliqué.

Fusible Web. I use a lightweight paper-backed fusible web, such as regular or Lite Steam-A-Seam 2, for all of my appliqué work. I like that there's paper backing on both sides of the fusible web on this product.

Stabilizer. Tear-away medium stabilizer is a must for machine appliqué. It helps you make smooth and even stitches.

Pins. I like to use curved basting pins when layering my quilt top, batting, and backing fabric in preparation for machine quilting.

Rotary Cutting

All of the projects in this book are designed for rotary cutting, and all the rotary-cutting measurements include ¼"-wide seam allowances. Cutting patchwork pieces with a rotary cutter is faster and more accurate than cutting them with scissors. Note that rotary-cutting instructions are written for right-handers; reverse the instructions if you are left-handed.

Cutting Straight Strips

1. Begin by pressing the fabric, then folding it in half lengthwise with the selvages aligned, wrong sides together. Place the fabric on your cutting mat with the folded edge nearest your body.

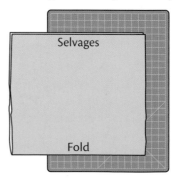

Selvages

Fold

2. Lay a 6" x 24" ruler on the right side of the fabric. Align a horizontal line of the ruler with the folded edge of the fabric. Position the ruler so that a little bit of each layer of your fabric extends beyond the side of the ruler. Cut along the long edge of the ruler. Discard the cut piece.

3. Rotate the fabric or mat so the straightened edge is to your left. Measuring from the straightened edge, cut strips to the width specified in the pattern instructions. For example, if you need 3"-wide strips, place the 3" vertical line of the ruler on the straightened edge of the fabric. Cut along the right side of the ruler.

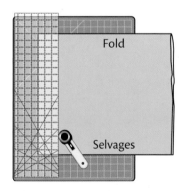

Fold

Selvages

Cutting Squares and Rectangles

1. Place a square ruler on the fabric and cut the first two sides of the square or rectangle.

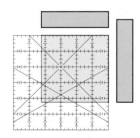

2. Turn the fabric around and line up the newly cut edges with the appropriate measurements on the ruler. Cut the remaining two sides of the square or rectangle.

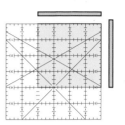

Machine Piecing

When sewing pieces together, always be sure to place the pieces right sides together and align the raw edges. The most important aspect of machine piecing is sewing an accurate ¼" seam allowance. This enables the seams to match and the blocks to fit together properly. Some machines have a special pressure foot that measures exactly ¼" from the center needle position to the edge of the foot. You can align the edge of your fabric with the edge of the presser foot, resulting in a perfect ¼" seam allowance. Some machines allow you to move the needle position to the right or left so that the resulting seam is ¼" away from the fabric edge to the stitching line.

If your machine doesn't have either of these features, you can create a seam guide. Place an accurate ruler under the presser foot and lower the needle onto the ¼" marking. Mark the seam allowance by placing a piece of masking tape at the edge of the ruler. Be careful not to cover the feed dogs on your sewing machine. Use several layers of masking tape, building a raised edge to guide your fabric. You can also use moleskin or a magnetic seam guide.

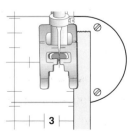

3

Making Templates

You'll need to make templates for some of the pieces in the projects. The template patterns are given with the projects that require them. All the patterns are full size, unless indicated otherwise. Depending on the technique used to stitch the pieces, the pattern may or may not include seam allowances. The seam allowance will be shown if it has been added and should be included when tracing the template. Seam allowances will not be added to the templates for appliqué pieces.

To make a template, follow these instructions.

1. Place a piece of template plastic, or the desired template material, over the pattern.

2. Use a fine-point permanent marker to trace the lines of the shape exactly onto the plastic. If the pattern has a fabric grain line, mark the line on the template. You may also want to write the pattern's identifying letter on the template.

3. Use utility scissors to cut out the template, cutting exactly on the drawn lines.

Fusible Appliqué

These directions will give you a basic knowledge of fusible appliqué. When you purchase a fusible-web product, take time to read the manufacturer's directions. Different products call for different heat settings and handling instructions. The appliqué shapes in this book have already been reversed for fusible appliqué.

1. Make plastic templates for each appliqué shape (see "Making Templates" above); then trace around each shape onto the paper-backing side of the fusible web as many times as needed for your project. If your project doesn't use repeated shapes, you can simply trace each shape directly from the pattern onto the paper side of the fusible web, eliminating the need to make plastic templates. If you need to make a reversed image, simply flip the template over and then trace around the shape.

2. Cut out each shape roughly ¼" outside the drawn line. Then trim out the center of the fusible-web shape, leaving at least ¼" inside the line. This will prevent your appliqué shapes from becoming too stiff once they're fused.

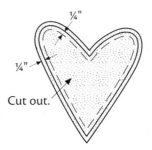

¼"

¼"

Cut out.

3. Place the fusible-web shapes on the wrong side of your appliqué fabric. Press, following the manufacturer's instructions.

Wrong side of fabric

4. Cut out the appliqué shapes directly on the drawn line.

5. Remove the paper backing from the shapes. Following the placement diagram for your particular project, position the appliqué shapes with the web-side down on the right side of the background fabric; press in place.

6. Cut a piece of tear-away stabilizer the same size as your background fabric. Pin the stabilizer to the wrong side of the background fabric centered under the appliqué design.

7. Machine stitch around the edge of the shape using a satin stitch. Remove the stabilizer after you have completed all of the machine stitching.

MAKING A SATIN STITCH

To make a satin stitch, set your sewing machine for a zigzag stitch and a shorter-than-normal stitch length. Aim for stitches that are closely spaced but that aren't so tightly formed that they overlap. The right swing of the needle should penetrate the background fabric; the left swing of the needle should go through the appliqué shape. Make sure all raw edges of the appliqué are covered.

To stitch an outside corner with overlapping zigzag stitches, stitch the first side of the shape, ending at the outside corner with the needle down in the background fabric at the outside edge of the appliqué. Raise the presser foot and pivot the fabric so you are ready to sew the next side. Lower the presser foot and resume stitching.

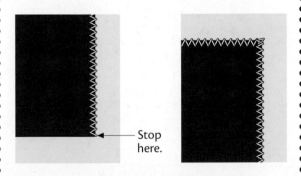

Stop here.

For both inner and outer curves, you'll need to pivot the fabric every few stitches to keep a smooth curve. The tighter the curve, the more frequently you'll need to pivot.

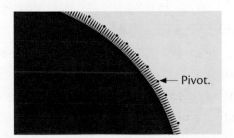

Pivot.

Pivot when the needle is outside of the appliqué shape.

Layering and Basting

When your quilt top is complete, measure its width and length. You will need batting and backing pieces that are at least 2" to 3" larger than the quilt top on all sides.

1. Lay your pressed backing, wrong side up, on a flat, clean surface. Anchor the backing with masking tape, taking care not to stretch the fabric out of shape. Center the batting over the backing, smoothing out any wrinkles.

2. Center the pressed quilt top, right side up, over the batting, smoothing out any wrinkles and making sure the edges of the quilt top are parallel to the edges of the backing.

3. For machine quilting, use curved basting pins to baste the three layers together. Starting in the center and working outward, place pins 3" to 4" apart over the entire quilt; try to avoid pinning areas where you intend to quilt. Finish by machine basting around the edges, about ⅛" from the edge of the quilt top. Note that if you are planning to quilt by hand, baste with a needle and thread.

Quilting

Once all the layers are basted together, you can quilt your project by hand or machine. Whichever method you choose to use, always select a design that will enhance your quilt. This can be straight-line quilting, free-motion quilting, or using a quilting stencil to quilt specific patterns. Be sure to start in the middle and work out to the edges to prevent any puckers or bunching.

When the quilting is complete, leave the basting stitches around the edges intact and remove any remaining pins. Trim the batting and backing even with the quilt top and make sure the corners are square.

Binding

The fabric requirements listed in this book for binding are based on using straight-grain binding strips cut 2½" wide and stitched to the outside edges of the quilt with a ¼" seam allowance.

1. Cut the number of binding strips indicated in the cutting instructions for your project. Cut the strips from selvage to selvage.

2. Stitch the strips together as shown to make one long continuous strip. Trim the excess fabric, leaving a ¼" seam allowance. Press the seams open.

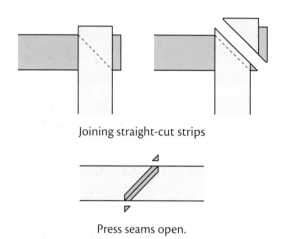

Joining straight-cut strips

Press seams open.

3. Fold back one end of the long binding strip ½" and press. Press the strip in half lengthwise, wrong sides together, with the raw edges aligned.

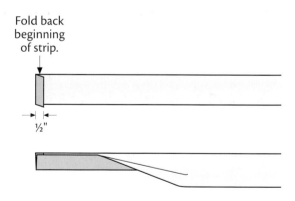

Fold back beginning of strip.

½"

4. Place the folded end of the binding strip in the middle of one side of your quilt. Line up the raw edges of the binding with the raw edge of the quilt. Using a walking foot and a ¼" seam allowance, begin stitching the binding to the quilt

top, 2" from the strip's folded end. Stop ¼" from the first corner and backstitch.

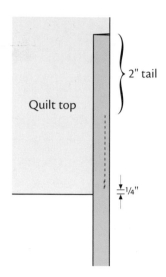

Quilt top

2" tail

¼"

5. Remove the quilt from the sewing machine. Fold the binding away from the quilt, and then fold it again and pin as shown to create an angled pleat at the corner. Begin with a backstitch at the fold of the binding and continue stitching along the edge of the quilt top. Repeat this process at each corner as you come to it.

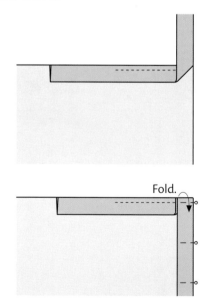

Fold.

6. When you are close to the beginning of the binding, stop 2" before the starting end and backstitch. Remove the quilt from the machine. Trim the binding tail ½" longer than needed and tuck the end inside the beginning strip. Pin in place, making sure the strip lies flat. Stitch the rest of the binding in place.

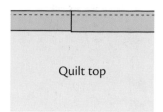

Quilt top

7. Turn the binding to the back of the quilt. Using thread to match the binding, hand stitch the binding in place so that the folded binding edge covers the row of machine stitching. At each corner, fold the binding to form a miter on the back of the quilt.

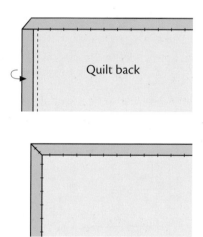

Quilt back

QUICK MACHINE BINDING

If you wish to avoid hand sewing the binding, and you don't mind if an extra row of stitching shows on the back of the quilt, try this quick machine method for binding.

1. After preparing the binding as described in steps 1–3 of "Binding" at left, sew the binding to the back of the quilt (rather than to the front) using a ¼" seam allowance and mitering the corners as usual.

2. Turn the binding to the front of the quilt and carefully pin the binding all around the perimeter, making sure to securely pin the corners. The binding should cover the machine stitches.

3. Sewing slowly and using thread that matches the binding, straight stitch along the folded edge of the binding on the right side of the quilt. You'll want to aim for a nice straight line of stitches. Do not sew through the mitered part of the corners; you can secure them with hand stitching if desired.

zinnia pincushion

What a pretty pincushion to accessorize your sewing space! This is a quick and easy design to make for holiday gifts, and the design possibilities are endless—use different felted wool and beads for an entirely different look.

Designed and made by Linda Lum DeBono
Finished size: 6½" long x 4½" wide x 3½" tall

Materials

- 6" x 15" piece of pink felted wool for flower petals
- 7" x 9" piece of light blue felted wool for pincushion sides
- 7" x 9" piece of lime green felted wool for pincushion top and bottom
- 6" x 6" square of moss green felted wool for leaves
- Embroidery floss: cream and colors to match wool and beads
- 80 light blue Maco beads for pincushion sides
- 14 pink cube-shaped beads for flower center
- 16 oz bag of polyester fiberfill
- Wave fabric shears or wavy-edged rotary-cutting blade for cutting leaves (optional)

Cutting

All measurements include ¼" seam allowances. The template pattern for piece E appears on page 21. For detailed instructions, refer to "Making Templates" (page 14).

From the lime green felted wool, cut:
2 pieces using pattern E

From the light blue felted wool, cut:
2 rectangles, 2½" x 7¼"

Assembling the Flower

1. Using patterns A–D (page 21) and the pink felted wool, cut out each flower shape. Layer the flower shapes, starting with the largest on the bottom and ending with the smallest on top.

2. Using a single strand of matching embroidery floss and stitching through all of the layers, sew the pink beads in the center of the flower.

Assembling the Pincushion

1. Referring to the photo (page 18) and using a single strand of matching embroidery floss, randomly hand sew the blue beads onto each 2½" x 7¼" rectangle.

2. Layer the rectangles with the beaded sides together and, using a ¼" seam allowance, sew along both short ends of the rectangles as shown to make the pincushion side.

3. Fold each lime green E piece in half lengthwise and lightly crease. Pin one lime green piece to one edge of the pincushion side, aligning the crease with the side seams of the rectangle. Using two strands of cream-colored embroidery floss, use a hand blanket stitch to sew the pieces together.

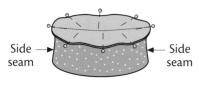 

Side seam → ← Side seam

4. Use pattern F (page 21) to cut out three moss green leaf shapes *or* use wave fabric shears to make three free-form leaves. Arrange the leaves and the flower on the lime green top as shown in the photo. Remove the flower; tack the base of

each leaf in place by hand. Reposition the flower. Stitching through all the layers, randomly hand stitch through the beads in the flower center to secure the flower to the lime green top.

Placement diagram

5. Repeating step 3, sew the remaining lime green E piece to the bottom of the pincushion using a blanket stitch. Stop stitching approximately 2" from the starting point to leave an opening for stuffing the pincushion. Firmly stuff the pincushion with polyester fiberfill.

6. Continue sewing a blanket stitch along the bottom of the pincushion to close the opening.

zinnia pincushion patterns

Patterns do not include
seam allowances.

B
Cut 1.

A
Cut 1.

C
Cut 1.

D
Cut 1.

E
Cut 2.

F
Cut 3.

cool girl's tool case

A companion to the pincushion, this tool case is made from gorgeous hand-dyed wools. Pamper yourself by making this to carry all of your little notions. It's a fabulous gift combination with the pincushion—and so fun and fast to whip up.

Designed and made by Linda Lum DeBono
Finished size: 9" x 13" (overall size)

Materials

Yardage is based on 42"-wide fabric.

11" x 15" piece of blue felted wool for cover

5" x 8" piece of red felted wool for flower petals

4" x 6" piece of pink felted wool for flower petals

75 lime green bugle beads for front cover

7 large round pink beads for flower center

½ yard of polka-dot print for lining

1 yard of ½"-wide black-and-white checked ribbon for ties

9" x 13" piece of heavyweight fusible interfacing

Embroidery floss: colors to match wool and beads

Cutting

All measurements include ¼" seam allowances.

From the blue felted wool, cut:
1 rectangle, 10" x 14"

From the polka-dot print, cut:
1 rectangle, 13½" x 22"
1 rectangle, 7½" x 13½"

From the checked ribbon, cut:
4 strips, 7½" long

Assembling the Cover

1. Center the interfacing, adhesive side down, on the wrong side of the blue felted wool rectangle. Following the manufacturer's instructions, press it with an iron.

2. Fold the edges of the wool rectangle over the outside edges of the interfacing to the non-adhesive side and press. Use a ¼" seam allowance and a thread color that matches the wool to sew all around the outside edge.

3. Using patterns A–D (page 25) and the pink and red felted wool, cut out each flower shape. Layer the flower shapes, starting with the largest on the bottom and ending with the smallest on top.

4. Referring to the placement diagram, position the layered flower on the front cover. Using a single strand of matching embroidery floss and stitching through all of the layers, including the interfacing, sew the large round beads in the center of the flower.

5. Using a single strand of matching embroidery floss, randomly hand sew the lime green bugle beads to the front of the cover.

Placement diagram

Making the Lining

1. With right sides together, fold the 13½" x 22" polka-dot rectangle in half as shown and press. Using a ¼" seam allowance, stitch each short end of the rectangle as shown, starting and ending with a backstitch. Leave the bottom edge open to turn the lining right side out. Turn the rectangle right side out and press.

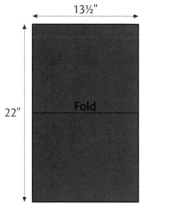

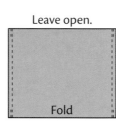

2. Position the rectangle from step 1 with the folded edge at the top. Fold the top folded edge over 1¾" again and press.

3. Repeating step 1, fold the 7½" x 13½" rectangle in half lengthwise and stitch each short end of the rectangle. Turn the rectangle right side out and press.

4. Position the smaller rectangle from step 3 on top of the larger rectangle from step 1 to create

a pocket, aligning the bottom raw edges of both rectangles together. Machine stitch a scant ¼" in from the raw edge.

5. Mark and topstitch a line down the center of the lining.

6. Mark and topstitch evenly spaced lines through the lower section of the lining to form separate pockets.

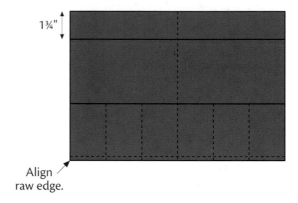

7. Along the bottom edge, turn the seam allowance of the lining under ¼" and press. Using a thread color that matches, sew a scant ¼" inside the outside edge around the lining.

8. Place the lining on the cover, covering the wool seam allowance and machine stitches. Tuck the pieces of ribbon between the lining and front cover, two on each side, 2" from the top and bottom edges as shown.

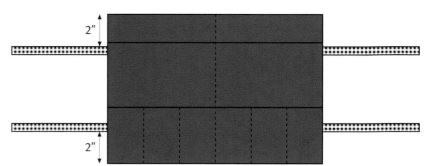

9. Stitch the lining in place using a blind stitch or slip stitch. Then topstitch down the center again, stitching through all the layers to make the spine of the case.

cool girl's tool case patterns

Patterns do not include seam allowances.

C
Cut 1.

B
Cut 1.

D
Cut 1.

A
Cut 1.

hip-hop case

Use this cool little case to protect the music player in your purse.

Designed and made by Linda Lum DeBono

Finished size: 3" × 5"

Materials

5" x 12" rectangle of pink felted wool for cover

5" x 12" rectangle of blue fabric for lining

5" x 5" square of brown tone-on-tone print for appliqué letters

5" x 5" square of fusible web

4" x 5" square of stabilizer

Cutting

All measurements include ¼" seam allowances.

From the pink felted wool, cut:
1 rectangle, 3½" x 10½"

From the blue fabric, cut:
1 rectangle, 3½" x 10½"

Appliquéing the Letters

1. Referring to "Fusible Appliqué" (page 14) and using the patterns at right and the brown tone-on-tone print, prepare and cut out the letter shapes. Fold the pink rectangle in half and lightly press. Unfold the pink rectangle and fuse the letters to the rectangle using the placement diagram.

2. Center and pin the stabilizer to the back of the pink rectangle.

3. Stitch around each letter using a satin stitch and matching thread.

4. Gently remove the stabilizer.

Placement diagram

Assembling the Case

1. Place the pink rectangle on top of the blue rectangle with right sides together. Using a ¼" seam allowance, sew each short end of the layered rectangles as shown. Press the seam allowances open.

2. With right sides together, align the seams as shown. Using a ¼" seam allowance, sew around the outside edges. Leave a 3" opening in the lining to turn the case right side out. Backstitch along each side of the opening.

Leave open.

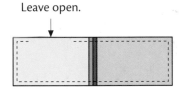

3. Clip the corners. Turn the case right side out and hand stitch the opening closed. Tuck the lining inside the completed case.

hip-hop case patterns

Patterns do not include seam allowances and are reversed for fusible appliqué.

pretty in pink pillow

Paisleys are hot. You see them everywhere, from bed sheets to stationery. This pillow is a great decorating accessory for your room. The felted wool gives it a homemade look while the colors add a lot of spunk.

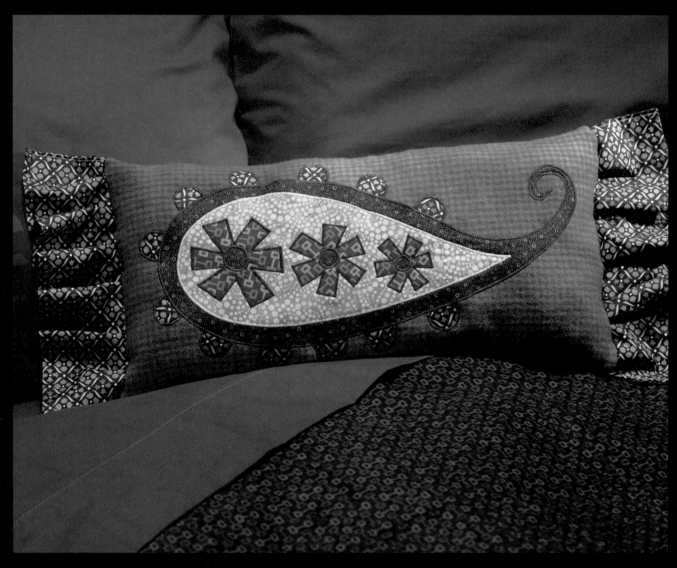

Designed and made by Linda Lum DeBono
Finished size: 9" x 25" including ruffle

Materials

Fat quarters measure 18" x 21".

1 fat quarter of pink houndstooth felted wool for pillow front

1 fat quarter of solid pink felted wool for pillow back

1 fat quarter of light pink print for paisley appliqué

1 fat quarter of dark pink print for appliqué flowers

1 fat quarter of chocolate tone-on-tone print for paisley appliqué and flower centers

1 fat quarter of chocolate-and-pink print for end ruffles and appliqué tabs

⅝ yard of fusible web

10" x 19" piece of stabilizer

16 oz bag of polyester fiberfill

Cutting

All measurements include ¼" seam allowances.

From the pink houndstooth felted wool, cut:
1 rectangle, 9½" x 19"

From the solid pink felted wool, cut:
1 rectangle, 9½" x 19"

From the chocolate-and-pink print, cut:
2 rectangles, 7" x 18"

Appliquéing the Pillow Top

1. Referring to "Fusible Appliqué" (page 14) and using patterns A–I (page 31), prepare the appliqué shapes. Using the appropriate fabrics, cut out each shape. Referring to the photo (page 30) for placement, fuse the shapes in order, starting with piece A, to the center of the 9½" x 19" pink houndstooth rectangle.

2. Center and pin the stabilizer to the back of the pink houndstooth rectangle.

3. Stitch around each shape using a satin stitch and matching thread.

4. Gently remove the stabilizer.

Assembling the Pillow

1. To make one ruffle, fold a 7" x 18" rectangle in half lengthwise, right sides together. Sew along each short end of the rectangle using a ¼" seam allowance. Turn the rectangle right side out; press. Topstitch ¼" in from each short end. Make two ruffles.

Fold

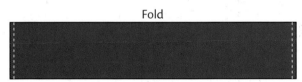

Make 2.

2. Using a longer stitch length, sew a gathering stitch the length of the ruffle, a scant ¼" in from the raw edge.

Stitch ¼" from raw edge.

3. Gather or pleat one ruffle, evenly adjusting the fullness, and place it on one short end of the pillow front. Matching the raw edges, position a ruffle ¼" in from the raw edge on each side of the pillow front as shown. Pin, and then stitch a scant ¼" in from the raw edges to secure the ruffles.

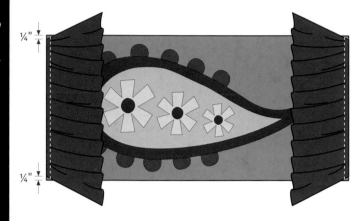

4. With the pillow front on top, place the front and back of the pillow right sides together and raw edges aligned. Being careful not to catch the ruffles in the seam, sew around the edges with a ¼" seam allowance. Leave a 3" opening along the bottom edge to turn the pillow right side out. Backstitch along each side of the opening.

5. Turn the pillow right side out. Stuff the pillow with fiberfill and close the opening with a slip stitch.

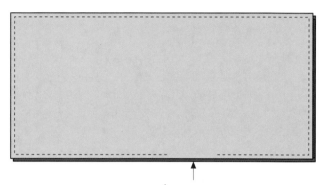

Leave open.

pretty in pink pillow patterns

Enlarge patterns 200%.
Patterns do not include seam allowances
and are reversed for fusible appliqué.

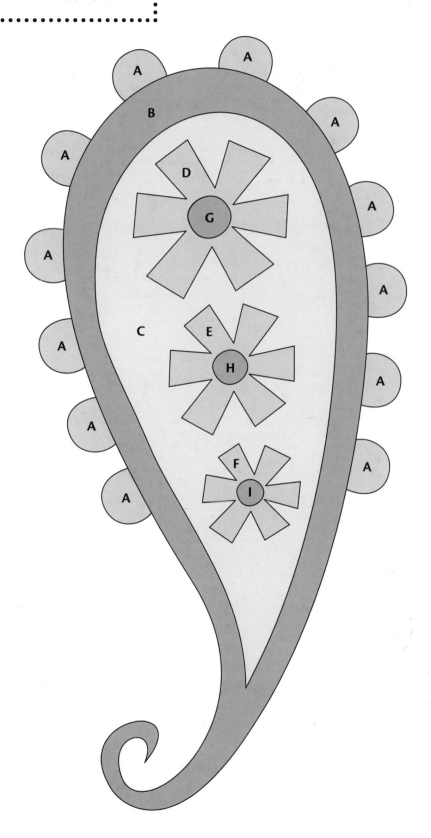

sticks of the trade needle case

I love my knitting accessories just as much as my finished knitted projects! Make this nifty knitting-needle case for those lovely needles of yours. The ruffle adds an extra special touch.

Designed and made by Linda Lum DeBono
Finished size: 14" x 20" including ruffle (overall size)

Materials

Yardages are based on 42"-wide fabrics. Fat eighths measure 9" x 21".

1 fat eighth *each* of 4 assorted light green floral prints for cover

½ yard of green paisley for ruffle

⅞ yard of fabric for lining

12½" x 16½" piece of heavyweight fusible interfacing

Cutting

All measurements include ¼" seam allowances.

From each of 3 of the assorted fat eighths, cut:
2 rectangles (6 total), 2½" x 11¼"

From the remaining fat eighth, cut:
1 rectangle, 5¾" x 12½"

From the green paisley, cut:
3 strips, 4½" x 42"

From the lining fabric, cut:
1 rectangle, 12½" x 16½"
1 rectangle, 12½" x 13"
1 rectangle, 6" x 12½"

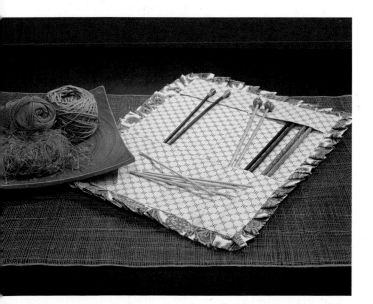

Assembling the Cover

1. Sew the six 2½" x 11¼" assorted rectangles together along the long edges to make the top section of the cover; press.

2. Sew the 5¾" x 12½" rectangle to one end of the unit as shown. Press.

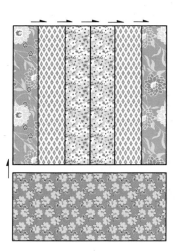

3. Place the interfacing, adhesive side down, on the wrong side of the cover. Following the manufacturer's instructions, press with an iron. On the right side, topstitch along the seam lines.

Making the Ruffle

1. Sew the 4½" x 42" green paisley strips together end to end to make one long strip. Join the two ends together to make a continuous loop.

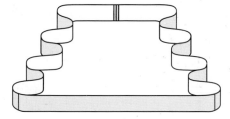

2. Fold the loop in half, wrong sides together and raw edges aligned. Press the folded edge.

Fold

3. Using a long stitch length, sew a gathering stitch the length of the ruffle, a scant ¼" in from the raw edge.

4. Gather or pleat the ruffle, evenly adjusting the fullness, and place it on top of the right side of the cover. Match the raw edges and pin around the outside edge as shown. Sew the ruffle to the edges of the case with a scant ¼" seam allowance.

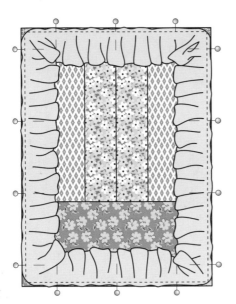

Align raw edges of cover and ruffle.
Pin. Stitch scant ¼" from edges.

Assembling the Lining

1. To make the bottom pocket, fold the 12½" x 13" lining rectangle in half, wrong sides together, and press. The folded rectangle should measure 12½" x 6½". Position the folded rectangle on top of the 12½" x 16½" lining rectangle, matching the raw edges, and pin in place.

2. Mark and stitch evenly spaced lines through the bottom part of the lining to form

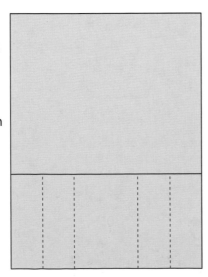

Topstitch.

the pockets. Note that you'll stitch the centerline in step 3.

3. To make the top pocket, fold the 6" x 12½" lining rectangle in half, wrong sides together, and press. The folded rectangle should measure 3" x 12½". Position the folded rectangle on the lining as shown. Matching the raw edges, pin and sew with a scant ¼" seam allowance. Then topstitch one long line through the center on top of both the top and bottom pockets; this will be the spine of the knitting case.

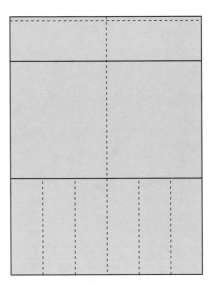

4. With the front cover on top, place the cover on the lining, right sides together. Sew around the edges with a ¼" seam allowance. Leave a 6" to 7" opening along one side to turn the case right side out. Backstitch along each side of the opening.

5. Trim the interfacing close to the stitching. Trim the corners and turn the case right side out. Close the opening with a slip stitch.

too cute to cook apron

If you're going to be a crafty girl, then you need a swell apron to look the part! This apron is functional, but don't be fooled—wearing this funky apron will make you feel like a crafty diva.

Designed and made by
Linda Lum DeBono
Finished size: 16½ " x 27½ "
(without ties)

Materials

Yardages are based on 42"-wide fabrics.

1 yard of large-scale floral print for pockets, ruffle, and ties

¾ yard of red tone-on-tone print for apron front

¾ yard of brown print for apron back and waistband

Cutting

All measurements include ¼" seam allowances.

From the large-scale floral print, cut:
1 rectangle, 14½" x 27½"
1 rectangle, 7½" x 40½"
2 rectangles, 5" x 32½"

From the red tone-on-tone print, cut:
1 rectangle, 16½" x 27½"

From the brown print, cut:
1 rectangle, 5" x 28½"
1 rectangle, 16½" x 27½"

Making the Apron Front

1. To make the ruffle, fold the 7½" x 40½" large-scale floral rectangle in half lengthwise, right sides together. Sew along each short end of the rectangle using a ¼" seam allowance. Turn the rectangle right side out; press. Topstitch ¼" in from each short end.

2. Place the short ends of the ruffle ¼" in from the outside edges of the 16½" x 27½" red rectangle as shown, right sides together. Match the raw edges. Evenly fold pleats across the width of the ruffle and stitch with a scant ¼" seam allowance.

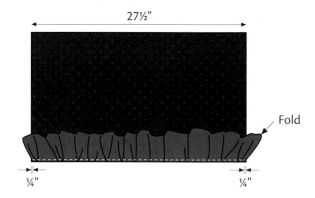

3. To make the pocket, fold the 14½" x 27½" large-scale floral rectangle in half lengthwise, right sides together. Using a ¼" seam allowance, sew along the long edge to make a tube. Turn the tube right side out and press.

4. Place the pocket on the center of the apron front as shown. Stitch with a scant ¼" seam allowance on each side.

5. Mark and sew two vertical lines 9" apart as shown to make the pockets. Topstitch along the bottom edge.

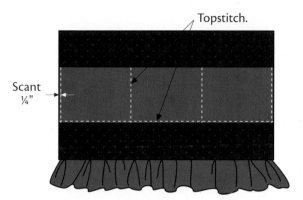

Topstitch.

Scant
¼"

Adding the Apron Back and Waistband

1. Place the apron front on top of the 16½" x 27½" brown rectangle, right sides together and raw edges aligned. Being careful not to catch the ruffle in the seams, sew along the side and bottom edges with a ¼" seam allowance. Leave the top open.

2. To make the waistband, fold the 5" x 28½" brown rectangle in half lengthwise, wrong sides together, and press.

3. Open the folded rectangle and center the rectangle along the top edge of the apron front, with right sides together and raw edges aligned. Stitch one raw edge of the waistband to the apron front and back with a ¼" seam allowance.

4. Fold under the seam allowance on each end ¼" and press. Turn the seam allowance along the long edge of the rectangle under ¼" and pin to the back of the waistband, covering the seam allowance and machine stitches. Stitch in place, leaving the ends open.

Making the Ties

1. Fold each 5" x 32½" rectangle in half lengthwise with right sides together and press.

2. Sew along the length of each tie and one short end with a ¼" seam allowance.

3. Turn each tie right side out and press.

4. Slightly pleat the open end of each tie and tuck a tie into each open side of the waistband. Topstitch each side to close the waistband and secure the ties.

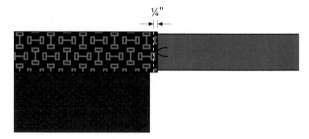

¼"

chrysanthemum sewing machine cover

No more vinyl or plastic here! Cover up your machine with this chic design.

Designed and made by Linda Lum DeBono
Finished size: 16" (wide) x 12" (tall) x 7½" (across)

Materials

Yardages are based on 42"-wide fabrics.

½ yard of large-scale tan floral print for front, back, and binding

⅓ yard of light blue toile print for gusset

1 fat quarter of light blue small-scale print for border

Scraps of solid brown fabric for appliqué letters

⅝ yard of brown print fabric for lining

3" x 10" piece of fusible web

3" x 10" piece of stabilizer

24" x 44" piece of batting

Cutting

All measurements include ¼" seam allowances. The dimensions of each piece below are based on a sewing machine that measures about 15" wide, 12" tall, and 7" across. You'll need to measure the size of your sewing machine and adjust the size of each piece accordingly.

From the large-scale tan floral print, cut:
2 strips, 2½" x 42"
2 rectangles, 8½" x 16½"

From the light blue toile print, cut:
1 rectangle, 8" x 32½"

From the light blue small-scale print, cut:
2 rectangles, 4½" x 16½"
2 rectangles, 4½" x 8"

From the brown print, cut:
2 rectangles, 8½" x 16½"
1 rectangle, 8" x 40½"

Making the Cover

1. Referring to "Fusible Appliqué" (page 14) and using the patterns (page 41) and the solid brown fabric, prepare and cut out the letter shapes. Using the placement diagram, fuse the letters to one 4½" x 16½" light blue rectangle.

2. Pin the stabilizer to the back of the rectangle.

3. Stitch around each letter using a satin stitch and matching thread.

4. Gently remove the stabilizer.

5. To make the front panel, sew the appliquéd rectangle to one long side of an 8½" x 16½" tan floral rectangle, right sides together; press. To make the back panel, sew the remaining light blue rectangle and tan floral rectangle together; press.

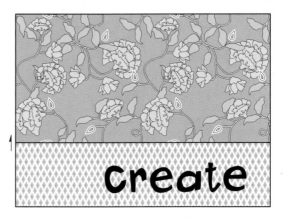

Placement diagram

6. To make the gusset, sew a 4½" x 8" light blue rectangle to each end of the 8" x 32½" blue toile rectangle; press.

7. Cut pieces of batting slightly larger than the front panel, the back panel, and the gusset. Layer each panel and the gusset with batting; baste the layers together. Quilt a curvy, meandering pattern over each piece.

8. Using the curved pattern at right, trim both top corners of the front panel and the back panel as shown. Trim any excess batting from all sides of both panels and the gusset.

Trim corners.

9. With right sides together, sew the front panel and the gusset together using a ¼" seam allowance. Then sew the back panel to the remaining side of the gusset. Turn the cover right side out.

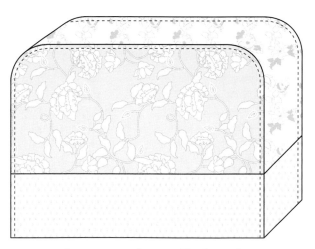

Sew gusset to front and back panels.

Making the Lining and Assembling the Cover

1. Using the curved pattern, trim both top corners of each 8½" x 16½" brown rectangle to make the front and back lining panels.

2. Sew the front and back lining panels to the 8" x 40½" brown rectangle as you did in step 9 of "Making the Cover" (at left).

3. With wrong sides together, tuck the lining inside the cover; pin and stitch a scant ¼" from the raw edges.

4. Referring to "Binding" (page 15), bind the bottom edge using the 2½" tan floral strips. Note that for this project, I folded the binding over the raw edges and topstitched the binding in place.

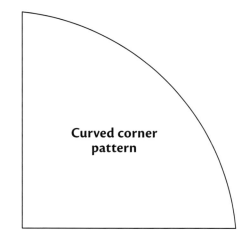

Curved corner pattern

chrysanthemum sewing machine cover patterns

Patterns do not include seam allowances and are reversed for fusible appliqué.

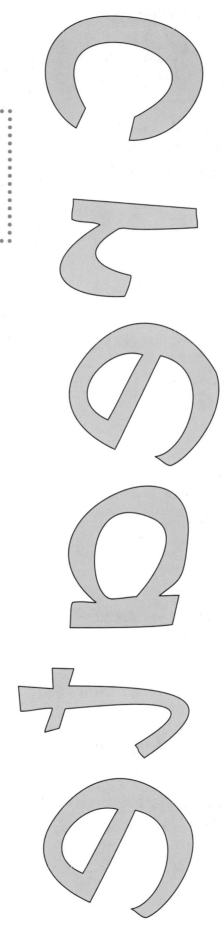

diamonds are a girl's best bag

If you are always on the run like I am and love to bring your projects along with you, then this is the bag for you. Carry your ongoing projects in style with this adorable bag.

Designed and made by Linda Lum DeBono
Finished dimensions: 16" × 20" (not including handles)

Materials

Yardages are based on 42"-wide fabrics.

¾ yard of brown tone-on-tone print for front, back, top, and bottom of bag

½ yard of green leaf print for front and back of bag

½ yard of brown floral print for front and back of bag

1 yard of brown print for lining

1 yard of heavyweight fusible interfacing

4" x 4" square of brown felt for bag tabs

2 pieces of batting, 18" x 22"

¾ yard of ¾"-wide flat braided leather trim

2 bag handles, 6½" wide at the base

4 bag feet, ½" diameter

Tracing paper

Cutting

All measurements include ¼" seam allowances. Template patterns for pieces A and B appear on page 45. For detailed instructions, refer to "Making Templates" (page 14).

From the green leaf print, cut:
8 diamonds using template A

From the brown floral print, cut:
10 diamonds using template A

From the brown tone-on-tone print, cut:
14 triangles using template B
1 rectangle, 5" x 26"
2 rectangles, 2½" x 12½"

From the leather trim, cut:
2 pieces, 10" long

Making the Front and Back Panels

1. Arrange four green A pieces, five brown floral A pieces, and seven brown tone-on-tone B pieces in diagonal rows as shown below in step 2.

2. Sew the pieces together in diagonal rows. Offset the points at the top edge ¼" as shown. Sew the rows together to make the front panel; press. Repeat steps 1 and 2 to make the back panel.

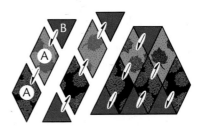

3. Cut two pieces of batting and two pieces of interfacing slightly larger than the front panel. With the adhesive side of the interfacing facing up, place the batting on top of the interfacing. Following the interfacing manufacturer's instructions, press with an iron. Then place the front panel on top of the batting, right side up, and pin in place. Repeat for the back panel.

4. Stitch along the seam lines through all three layers to quilt both the front and back panels. Trim any excess batting and interfacing even with the edges of the front panel. Repeat to trim the back panel.

5. Trace the outline of the front panel onto a piece of tracing paper to make a paper template. (You'll use this in step 4 of "Assembling the Bag" to cut out the lining pieces.)

6. Fold each 2½" x 12½" brown tone-on-tone rectangle in half lengthwise and press. With right sides together and raw edges aligned, sew one raw edge of the folded rectangle to the top edge of the front panel using a ¼" seam allowance. Repeat to sew a folded rectangle to the top edge of the back panel.

Making the Bottom of the Bag

1. To make a template for the bag bottom, start by drawing a 4" x 16" rectangle onto tracing paper.

2. On each short end, measure down 2" and place a mark to indicate the center of the rectangle. From one center mark, measure over 4" to the outside of the rectangle and place another mark. To make a triangle, draw lines from the second mark to the corner of the rectangle as shown. Repeat to make a triangle at each end of the rectangle. Then add a ¼" seam allowance to all sides of the template.

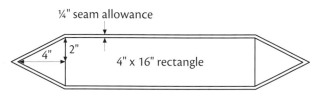

¼" seam allowance

4" 2"

4" x 16" rectangle

Bag bottom template

3. Use the template from step 2 to cut out one bottom piece from the 5" x 26" brown rectangle and one piece of interfacing. Fuse the interfacing to the wrong side of the bottom piece.

Assembling the Bag

1. With right sides together, sew the bottom edge of the front panel and the long side of the bottom piece together as shown. Sew the back panel to the other long side of the bottom piece.

2. On the right side of the front panel only, sew the leather trim to each of the upper side edges using a scant ¼" seam allowance. With right sides

together, sew the front and back panels to the bottom piece along the side seams, backstitching at the top edge as shown. Repeat for the other side of the bag.

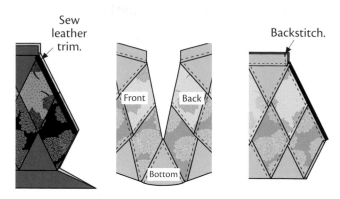

Sew leather trim.

Front Back

Bottom

Backstitch.

3. Add the feet to the bottom piece following the manufacturer's directions. Turn the bag right side out.

4. Using the template from step 5 of "Making the Front and Back Panels" (page 43) and the template for the bottom piece, trace and cut out two panels and one bottom piece from the lining fabric. Repeat steps 1 and 2 to sew the pieces together (but you won't be sewing the leather trim to the lining).

5. Place the lining inside the bag, wrong sides together and top edges aligned. Baste the lining and the bag together along the top edge of the lining.

6. Turn the seam allowance of the folded rectangle under ¼" as shown. Pin the folded edge to the bag lining, covering all of the raw edges and stitching line. Hand stitch in place.

7. Fold the rectangle in half again, align the folded edges on the inside of the bag, and topstitch in place by stitching around the top of the bag along the folded edge.

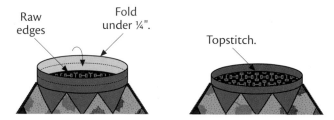

Raw edges

Fold under ¼".

Topstitch.

8. Measure the width of the opening at the base of the handles. From the brown felt square, cut four rectangles to fit that width. Insert the felt rectangles into the handle opening and sew the handles to the top of the front and back of the bag as shown.

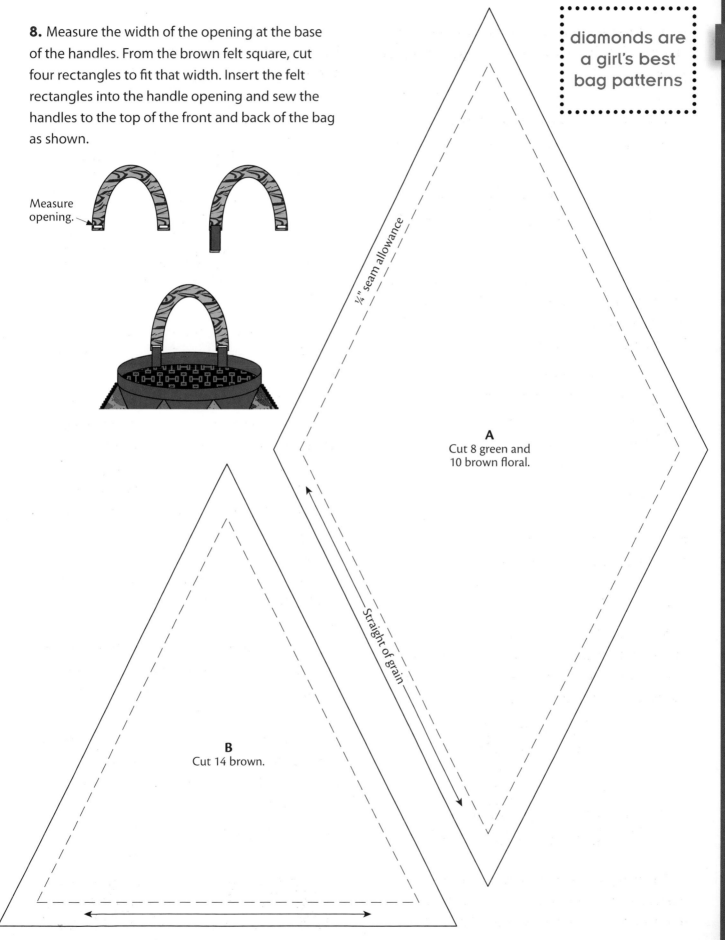

Measure opening.

¼" seam allowance

Straight of grain

A
Cut 8 green and 10 brown floral.

B
Cut 14 brown.

diamonds are a girl's best bag patterns

party it up coasters

Crafty girls love to have friends over for fun parties. Why not add some bright spots to your party decor with these funky little coasters?

Designed and made by Linda Lum DeBono

Finished size: 4" diameter

Materials

Yields 9 coasters.

18–22 scraps, each at least 5" x 5", of assorted purple, aqua, lime green, light green, orange, pink, and fuchsia prints for coasters and appliqué

9 squares, 5" x 5", of batting

½ yard or 9 squares, 5" x 5", of fusible web

9 squares, 5" x 5", of stabilizer

Making the Coasters

1. Referring to "Making Templates" (page 14), trace the circle pattern (page 48) onto template plastic and cut out the circle, including the seam allowance. Using the plastic circle template and the 5" squares of fabric, cut out 18 circles for the fronts and backs of the coasters. Set aside 9 circles for the back of the coasters.

2. Referring to "Fusible Appliqué" (page 14) and using the patterns (page 49), prepare the appliqué shapes. Referring to the photo at left and using the assorted prints, cut out each shape. Using nine of the circles from step 1, fuse an appliqué shape in the center of each circle.

3. Center and pin a piece of stabilizer to the back of each circle.

4. Stitch around each shape using a satin stitch and matching thread.

5. Gently remove the stabilizer.

6. Using the plastic circle template from step 1, cut out nine circles of batting.

CREATE YOUR OWN INITIAL

I made a coaster with my initial (L), but you may want to use your own initial. To make a pattern of your own initial, start by finding a font on your computer that you like. Then increase the size of the font to 72 or even larger. You can also enlarge the letter on a photocopier. Then prepare the letter shape for appliqué as described in step 2.

7. With right sides together, place each appliqué circle on top of a back circle, and then layer with a batting circle on the bottom. Baste the layers together.

8. Stitch around the outside edge of the circle sandwich using a ¼" seam allowance. Leave a 2½" opening to turn the circles right side out. Backstitch along each side of the opening. Trim the batting close to the stitching line.

9. Turn the circles right side out. Close the opening with a slip stitch.

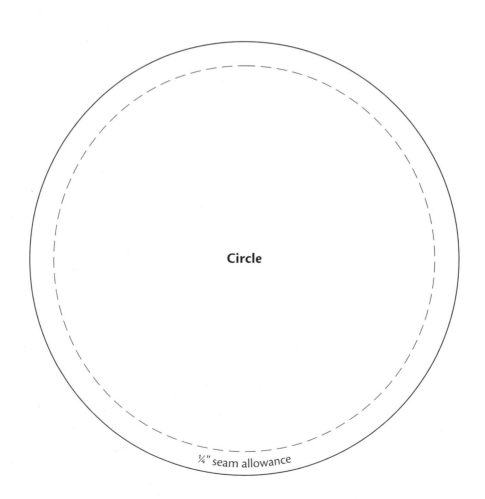

Circle

¼" seam allowance

party it up coasters patterns

Appliqué patterns do not include seam allowances and are reversed for fusible appliqué.

daisies in the sky pennants

Decorate a room with these adorable pennants. They're easy to make and are a great gift.

Designed and made by Linda Lum DeBono
Finished size: each pennant is 6½" x 7"

Materials

Yields 7 pennants. Yardages are based on 42"-wide fabrics.

14–22 scraps, each at least 8" x 8", of assorted light blue, yellow, brown, and red fabrics for pennants and flower appliqués

¼ yard of teal print for tie

16" x 32" piece of batting

½ yard of fusible web

7 squares, 6" x 6", of stabilizer

Cutting

Measurements include ¼" seam allowances.

From the teal print, cut:
2 strips, 2½" x 42"

Making the Pennants

1. Referring to "Making Templates" (page 14), trace the pennant pattern (page 53) onto template plastic and cut out the pattern, including the seam allowance. Using the plastic template and the 8" squares of fabric, cut out 14 pennant shapes. Set 7 aside for the backs of the pennants.

2. Referring to "Fusible Appliqué" (page 14) and using the daisy and flower-center patterns (page 53), prepare the appliqué shapes. Referring to the photo at left and using the assorted prints, cut out the appliqué shapes. Fuse a daisy to the center of each pennant front, and then fuse the flower center to the daisy.

3. Center and pin a piece of stabilizer to the back of each pennant.

4. Stitch around each shape using a satin stitch and matching thread.

5. Gently remove the stabilizer.

6. Using the plastic template from step 1, cut out seven pennant shapes from the batting.

7. With right sides together, place each appliqué pennant on top of a back pennant, and then layer with a batting pennant on the bottom. Baste the layers together.

8. Stitch around the outside edge of each pennant sandwich using a ¼" seam allowance. Leave the straight side open to turn the pennants right side out. Backstitch along each side of the opening.

9. Trim the batting close to the stitching line. Turn the pennants right side out. Outline stitch around each daisy shape and flower center.

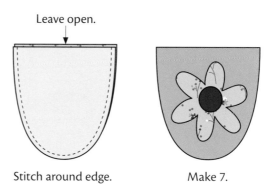

Leave open.

Stitch around edge.   Make 7.

Making the Tie

1. Sew the two 2½" x 42" teal strips together end to end to make one long strip.

2. Press the strip in half lengthwise, wrong sides together and raw edges aligned.

Assembling the Pennants and Tie

1. Fold the tie in half and mark the center with a pin. Fold one pennant in half and lightly crease to mark the center. With raw edges aligned and matching the center marks, place the pennant on top of the tie as shown and pin. Arrange three pennants on each side of the center pennant, spacing the pennants 1½" apart. Pin and then sew one raw edge along the top of each pennant with a ¼" seam allowance.

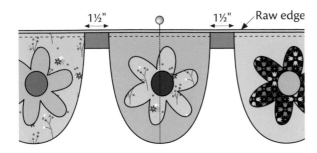

2. Press the seam allowance toward the strip, including the seam allowance in the space between the pennants. Along the raw edge of the entire length of the strip, fold and press a ¼" seam allowance.

3. Position the folded strip as shown so that the folded edges are aligned and the stitching along the top of the pennants is covered. Topstitch along the entire length of the tie using matching thread.

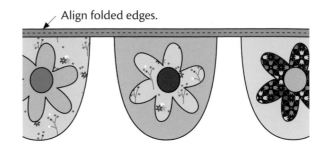

4. Place a knot at each end of the tie.

daisies in the sky pennants patterns

Appliqué patterns do not include seam allowances and are reversed for fusible appliqué.

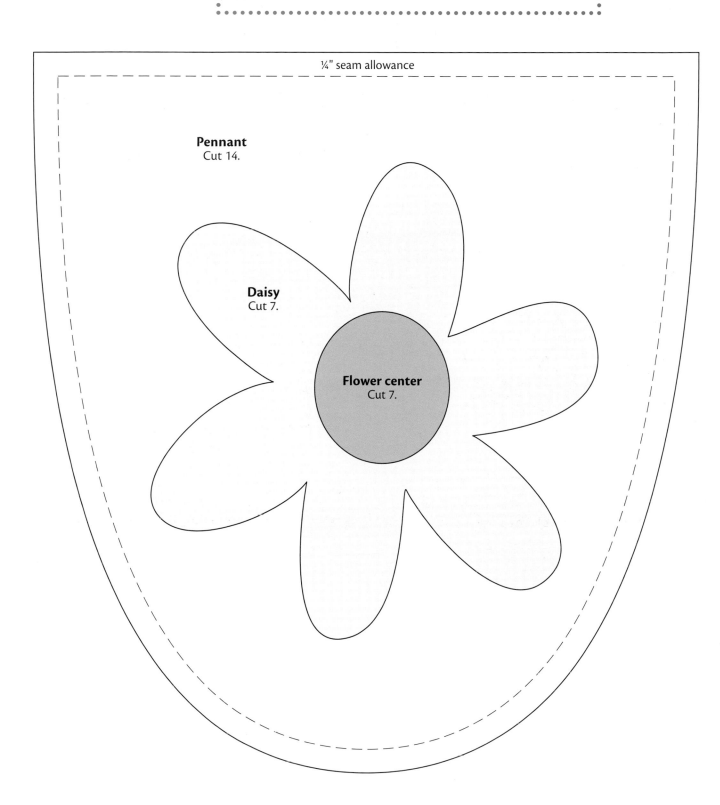

¼" seam allowance

Pennant
Cut 14.

Daisy
Cut 7.

Flower center
Cut 7.

flowers in my garden table runner

Your table never looked so fine! Your guests will love this cute and colorful table runner.

Pieced and quilted by Linda Lum DeBono

Finished size: 13¾" × 44¼"

Materials

Yardages are based on 42"-wide fabrics.

2 yards of purple print for block sashing, flower centers, binding, and backing

⅝ yard of multicolored swirl print for table-runner background

¼ yard of green tone-on-tone print for appliqué backgrounds

¼ yard of pink print for flower appliqués

¼ yard of oval print for center strip

¼ yard of fusible web

17" x 48" piece of batting

3 squares, 6" x 6", of stabilizer

Cutting

Measurements include ¼" seam allowances. Cut pieces in the order listed.

From the multicolored swirl print, cut:
8 rectangles, 5¼" x 5¾"
6 rectangles, 3" x 8¾"

From the oval print, cut
4 rectangles, 3¼" x 5¼"

From the green tone-on-tone print, cut:
3 squares, 6¼" x 6¼"

From the purple print, cut:
1 strip, 17" x 48", cut on the lengthwise grain
4 strips, 2½" x 42"
3 strips, 1¾" x 42"; crosscut into 6 strips, 1¾" x 8¾", and 6 strips, 1¾" x 6¼"

Assembling the Rows

This table runner consists of two repeating rows. The A rows are made of three rectangles each. The B rows feature flower-appliqué blocks.

Row A

1. Sew a 5¼" x 5¾" swirl-print rectangle and a 3¼" x 5¼" oval-print rectangle together. Press the seam allowance toward the swirl print.

2. Sew a second 5¼" x 5¾" swirl print to the opposite side of the oval-print piece. Press the seam allowance toward the swirl print. The unit should be 13¾" x 5¼".

3. Repeat steps 1 and 2 to make a total of four A rows.

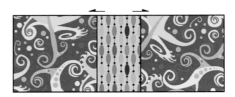

Row A.
Make 4.

Row B

1. Referring to "Fusible Appliqué" (page 14) and using the daisy and flower-center patterns (page 57) and the pink and purple prints, prepare and cut out the appliqué shapes. Fuse a daisy to the center of each 6¼" green square; then fuse a flower center to the top of the daisy. Make a total of three blocks.

2. Center and pin a piece of stabilizer to the back of each square.

3. Stitch around each shape using a satin stitch and matching thread.

4. Gently remove the stabilizer.

5. Sew a 1¾" x 6¼" purple strip to the left and right sides of each block. Press the seam allowances toward the purple strips.

6. Sew a 1¾" x 8¾" purple strip to the bottom and top of each block. Press the seam allowances toward the purple strips.

7. Sew a 3" x 8¾" swirl-print rectangle to the left and right sides of each block. Press the seams toward the swirl print. Each unit should measure 13¾" x 8¾".

Row B.
Make 3.

Joining the Rows

Sew one row A to one row B. Press the seams toward row A. Then add the next row A. Continue in this manner until you've sewn all the rows together as shown. The assembled table-runner top should measure 13¾" x 44¼".

Assembly diagram

Finishing the Table Runner

1. Layer the table runner top with the batting and backing (the 17" x 48" purple print piece); baste the layers together.

2. Quilt as desired. I machine quilted around each appliqué shape and then quilted the background with meandering circles and swirls. Referring to "Binding" (page 15), bind the table runner using the 2½"-wide purple strips.

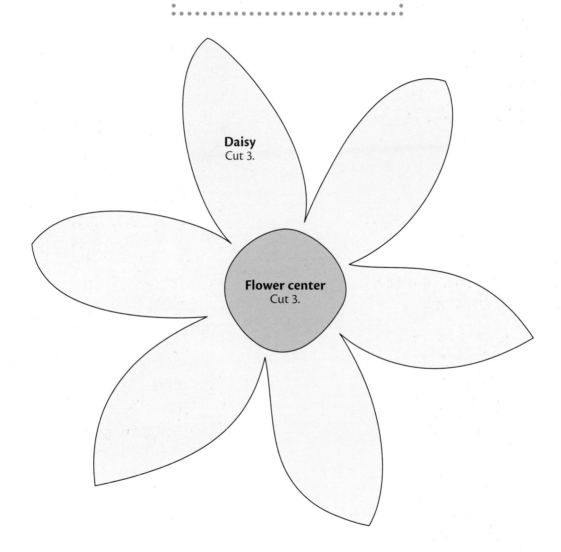

flowers in my garden
table runner patterns

Patterns do not include seam
allowances and are reversed
for fusible appliqué.

Daisy
Cut 3.

Flower center
Cut 3.

cover me pretty book cover

Dress up your boring school books with this stylish cover. Mix and match different fabrics for a funky look. Don't be afraid to use fabric combinations in different scales for that "wow!" effect.

Designed and made by Linda Lum DeBono

Finished size: 10" x 15" (overall size)

Materials

Yardages are based on 42"-wide fabrics.

¼ yard of chocolate swirl fabric for front cover and inside flaps

6 scraps, each at least 4" x 6", of assorted light green and brown floral prints for front cover

⅜ yard of brown floral fabric for lining

Cutting

Measurements include ¼" seam allowances.

From the assorted scraps, cut:
6 rectangles, 3" x 5½"

From the chocolate swirl fabric, cut:
1 rectangle, 5½" x 15½"
2 rectangles, 3½" x 10½"

From the brown floral, cut:
1 rectangle, 10½" x 21½"

Making the Cover

1. Sew the six 3" x 5½" assorted rectangles together along the long edges to make the top section of the cover. Press the seam allowances in one direction.

2. Sew the 5½" x 15½" chocolate swirl rectangle to one end of the section from step 1. Press as shown below.

3. Sew a 3½" x 10½" chocolate swirl rectangle to each side of the unit from step 2 as shown.

Assembling the Cover

1. Place the front cover on top of the 10½" x 21½" brown floral rectangle, right sides together and raw edges aligned. Pin the layers together.

2. Sew around the edges with a ¼" seam allowance. Leave a 3" opening to turn the cover right side out. Backstitch along each side of the opening.

3. Turn the cover right side out and press. Close the opening with a slip stitch.

4. On each end, fold the 3"-wide chocolate swirl rectangle to the inside and then hand stitch the front and back together along the top and bottom edges as shown to make pockets.

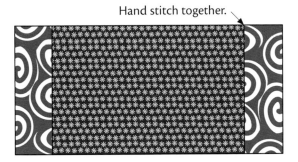

Hand stitch together.

5. On the front side, pin the two layers together and then topstitch down the center as shown.

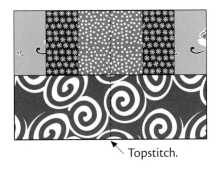

Topstitch.

best friends pillow sham

Every girl loves to have a party. Make this pillow sham in different fabrics for different recipients—bright and happy for a child, or in darker colors for dorm-room decor.

Designed and made by Linda Lum DeBono
Finished size: 27" x 32½"

Materials

Yardages are based on 42"-wide fabrics.

1⅜ yards of red paisley fabric for front border and pillow back

⅔ yard of yellow fabric for appliqué background

¼ yard of pink fabric for appliqué letters

⅓ yard of fusible web

20" x 26" piece of stabilizer

20" x 26" pillow form or standard bed pillow

Cutting

Measurements include ¼" seam allowances.

From the yellow print, cut:
1 rectangle, 20½" x 26"

From the red paisley fabric, cut:
4 strips, 4" x 38"
2 rectangles, 18½" x 27½"

Appliquéing the Pillow Sham

1. Referring to "Fusible Appliqué" (page 14) and using the patterns (pages 62 and 63) and the pink fabric, prepare and cut out the letter shapes. Referring to the photo at left, fuse the letters to the yellow print rectangle.

2. Center and pin the stabilizer to the back of the rectangle.

3. Stitch around each letter using a satin stitch and matching thread.

4. Gently remove the stabilizer.

Making the Pillow Front

1. Mark the center of the yellow rectangle on each side. Mark the center of each 4" x 38" paisley strip.

2. With right sides together, sew the strips to the yellow rectangle with a ¼" seam allowance, matching the centers. Start and stop stitching ¼" from the edge of the rectangle. Press all seam allowances toward the paisley strips. The strips should extend beyond the rectangle at each end.

3. Lay one corner of the sham on your ironing board as shown. Fold under one strip at a 45° angle to the other strip. Press and pin.

4. Fold the pillow front, right sides together, and line up the edges of the border strips. Stitch along the pressed crease, sewing from the inner corner to the outer edge. Trim the seam allowance to ¼" and press the seam open. Miter the remaining corners in the same manner.

Pressed crease

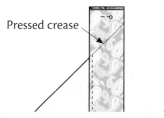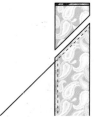

Assembling the Pillow Sham

1. To make the pillow back, fold over ¼" on one 18½" edge of both red paisley rectangles, and then fold over ¼" again. Press and machine stitch along the folded edge.

2. Overlap the pillow backs on top of the pillow front, right sides together, as shown. Pin and then stitch using a ¼" seam allowance.

3. Clip the corners and turn the pillow sham right side out; press.

4. Topstitch along the seam line on all sides to form a flange. Insert the pillow form through the opening.

Overlap

Topstitch

Best friends

best friends pillow sham patterns

Patterns do not include seam allowances and are reversed for fusible appliqué.

"hi" and heart greeting cards

I love handmade greeting cards, and I love to use up my scraps. These cards fit the bill, and you can add your own personal touch by choosing the right fabrics for the right occasions. Use leftover scraps from your projects to whip up these fun little cards in no time!

Pieced and quilted by Linda Lum DeBono
Finished size: 5" x 5" each

Materials

"Hi" Card:

5" x 10" piece of lime green card stock for card base

4¾" x 4¾" square of lime green card stock for inside lining of card

4¼" x 4¼" square of brown fabric for background

3½" x 3½" square of green felted wool for appliqué background

Scraps of brown fabrics for appliqué

Heart Card:

5" x 10" piece of blue card stock for card base

4¾" x 4¾" square of blue card stock for inside lining of card

4¼" x 4¼" square of pink fabric for background

3½" x 3½" square of blue felted wool for appliqué background

Scrap of pink fabric for appliqué

For Both Designs:

2 squares, 4¼" x 4¼", of fusible web

2 squares, 3½" x 3½", of fusible web

2 squares, 3½" x 3½", of stabilizer

Pinking shears or wavy-edged rotary blade

Scoring tool

Pressing cloth

All-purpose glue or square adhesive tabs

Assembling the Cards

1. Referring to "Fusible Appliqué" (page 14) and using the patterns (page 66), prepare and cut out the pink heart and brown letter shapes. Fuse the heart shape to the 3½" blue felted-wool square and the letter shapes to the 3½" green felted-wool square.

2. Center and pin a piece of stabilizer to the back of each square.

3. Stitch around each shape using a satin stitch and matching thread.

4. Gently remove the stabilizer.

5. Apply fusible web to back of each appliquéd square. Trim the edges of the square with pinking shears.

FOLDING CARD STOCK

For perfectly straight creases, lay a ruler along the desired fold line; then run a scoring tool along the ruler's edge to score the card.

---

6. Apply fusible web to the wrong side of the 4¼" pink and brown squares. Fold each 5" x 10" piece of card stock in half to make a 5" x 5" card. Using a dry iron and a pressing cloth to protect the card, center and fuse the pink fabric square to the blue card front and the brown fabric square to the lime green card front. Stitch around each square with a satin stitch and matching thread.

7. Center and fuse the blue appliquéd wool square from step 5 to the blue card front; again use a dry iron and pressing cloth. Center and fuse the green appliquéd wool square to the green card front.

8. Center and glue a 4¾" piece of card stock to the inside of each card front to cover up the machine stitches.

"hi" and heart greeting cards patterns

Patterns do not include seam allowances and are reversed for fusible appliqué.

love

Tell someone that you love her with this adorable little quilt. This quilt has lots of small pieces, but is easy to make. The colors twinkle and will light up any room for that special someone.

Pieced and quilted by Linda Lum DeBono

Finished size: 21½" x 31½"

Materials

Yardages are based on 42"-wide fabrics.

¼ yard *each* of 9 to 10 different purple, fuchsia, yellow, turquoise, and green tone-on-tone prints for appliqué-block backgrounds and appliqué shapes

¼ yard *each* **or** scraps, each at least 6" x 8", of 6 to 7 different yellow, purple, green, and fuchsia small-scale prints for plain blocks

⅜ yard of black-and-white print for binding

1 yard of fabric for backing

25" x 35" piece of batting

1 yard of fusible web

1 yard of stabilizer

Cutting

Measurements include ¼" seam allowances.

From the assorted tone-on-tone prints, cut a *total* of:
4 rectangles, 4" x 5½"
3 rectangles, 4" x 6"
5 rectangles, 4½" x 5"
1 rectangle, 4¾" x 9"
8 squares, 5" x 5"
4 squares, 5¼" x 5¼"

From the assorted small-scale prints, cut*:
2 rectangles, 4" x 5"
2 rectangles, 4¾" x 8"
2 rectangles, 5½" x 6"
2 rectangles, 3" x 5¼"
2 rectangles, 4" x 6"
2 rectangles, 4" x 5"
1 rectangle, 3" x 5"

These pieces are for the plain blocks at the end of each row and are listed in the order needed for each row, starting with row 1 at the top and ending with row 7.

From the black-and-white print, cut:
4 strips, 2½" x 42"

From the stabilizer, cut:
4 rectangles, 4" x 5½"
3 rectangles, 4" x 6"
5 rectangles, 4½" x 5"
1 rectangle, 4¾" x 9"
8 squares, 5" x 5"
4 squares, 5¼" x 5¼"

Appliquéing the Blocks

1. Referring to "Fusible Appliqué" (page 14) and using the patterns (pages 70 and 71), prepare the flower, heart, and letter shapes. Referring to the photo (page 67) and using the assorted tone-on-tone prints, cut out each shape.

2. Fuse each flower A shape, and then a flower A center, to the middle of a 5" tone-on-tone print square. Make four flower A blocks.

3. Fuse the *l, o, v,* and *e* letters to the center of the 4¾" x 9" tone-on-tone print rectangle.

4. Fuse each heart A shape to a 4" x 5½" tone-on-tone print rectangle. Make four heart A blocks.

5. Fuse each flower B shape, and then a flower B center, to the middle of a 5¼" tone-on-tone print square. Make four flower B blocks.

6. Fuse each XO shape to the center of a 4" x 6" tone-on-tone print rectangle. Make three XO blocks.

7. Fuse each flower C shape, and then a flower C center, to the middle of a 5" tone-on-tone print square. Make four flower C blocks.

8. Fuse each heart B shape to a 4½" x 5" tone-on-tone print rectangle. Make five heart B blocks.

9. Using a piece of stabilizer the same size as the block, center and pin the stabilizer to the back of each block.

10. Stitch around each shape using a satin stitch and matching thread.

11. Gently remove the stabilizer.

Assembling the Quilt

This quilt consists of seven different rows. Each row is made with repeating appliqué blocks and plain blocks to complete the row.

Row 1

Sew four flower A blocks together to make a horizontal row. Sew a 4" x 5" rectangle to each end of the row. Press the seam allowances in one direction.

Row 2

Sew the *love* block between two 4¾" x 8" rectangles. Press the seam allowances toward the rectangles.

Row 3

Sew four heart A blocks together to make a horizontal row. Sew a 5½" x 6" rectangle to each end of the row. Press the seam allowances in one direction.

Row 4

Sew four flower B blocks together to make a horizontal row. Sew a 3" x 5¼" rectangle to each end of the row. Press the seam allowances in one direction.

Row 5

Sew three *XO* blocks together to make a horizontal row. Sew a 4" x 6" rectangle to each end of the row. Press the seam allowances in one direction.

Row 6

Sew four flower C blocks together to make a horizontal row. Sew a 4" x 5" rectangle to each end of the row. Press the seam allowances in one direction.

Row 7

Sew five heart B blocks together to make a horizontal row. Sew a 3" x 5" rectangle to one end of the row. Press the seam allowances in one direction.

Joining the Rows

Refer to the assembly diagram to arrange the rows, shifting the rows from left to right as desired. Starting with row 1, sew row 1 to row 2. Press the seams toward row 2. Continue in this manner until you've sewn all the rows together as shown. Use a ruler and rotary cutter to trim the assembled quilt to measure 21½" x 31½".

Assembly diagram

Finishing the Quilt

1. Layer the quilt top with the batting and then the backing; baste the layers together.

2. Quilt as desired. I machine quilted around each appliqué shape, and then quilted the background with meandering lines, loops, and swirls. Referring to "Binding" (page 15), bind the quilt using the 2½"-wide black-and-white strips.

love patterns

Patterns do not include seam allowances and are reversed for fusible appliqué.

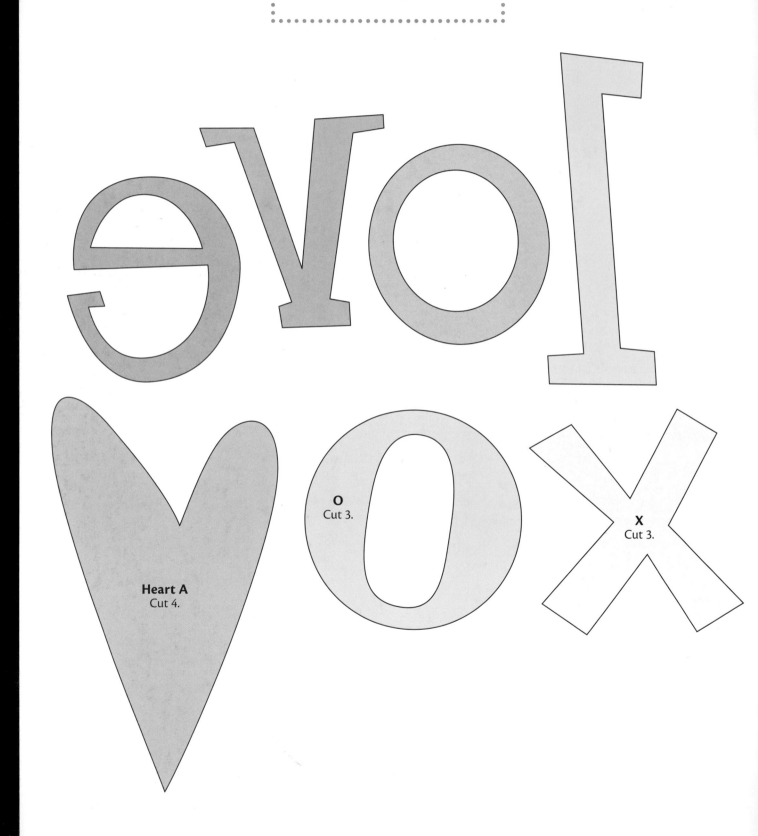

Heart A
Cut 4.

O
Cut 3.

X
Cut 3.

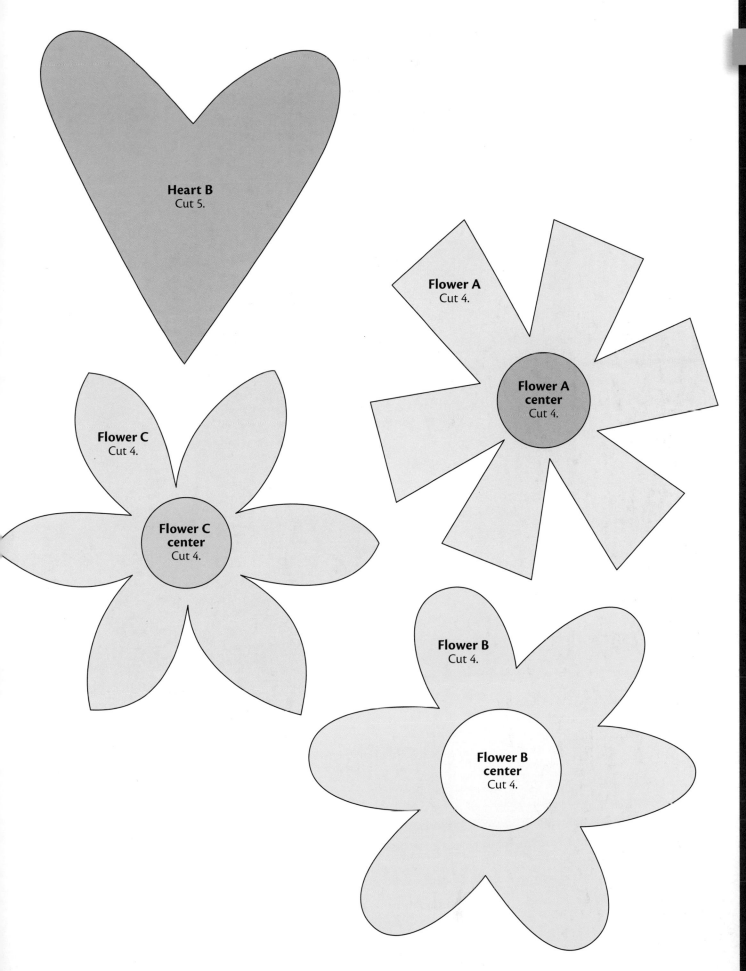

Heart B
Cut 5.

Flower A
Cut 4.

Flower A center
Cut 4.

Flower C
Cut 4.

Flower C center
Cut 4.

Flower B
Cut 4.

Flower B center
Cut 4.

bohemian flourish

Add a little Bohemian flair to your room. The colors are exotic and the pleats are fun and girly.

Pieced and quilted by Linda Lum DeBono

Finished size: 30½" x 42½"

Materials

Yardages are based on 42"-wide fabrics.

½ yard *each* of 1 orange, 2 brown, and 2 gold solid-colored fabrics for pleated blocks, appliqué-block backgrounds, and flower appliqués

½ yard *each* of 1 orange, 1 gold, and 2 brown prints for pleated blocks and flower appliqués

⅜ yard of brown fabric for binding

1½ yards of backing fabric

35" x 47" piece of batting

1 yard of fusible web

1¼ yards of stabilizer

Cutting

Measurements include ¼" seam allowances.

From the orange, brown, and gold solid-colored fabrics, cut a *total* of:
5 rectangles, 10½" x 14½"
16 strips, 5½" x 15½"

From the orange, gold, and brown prints, cut a *total* of:
16 rectangles, 5½" x 7½"

From the brown fabric for binding, cut:
4 strips, 2½" x 42"

From the stabilizer, cut:
5 rectangles, 10½" x 14½"

Appliquéing the Blocks

1. Referring to "Fusible Appliqué" (page 14) and using the patterns (pages 76 and 77), prepare the flower shapes. Using the solid and printed fabrics, cut out each shape. Referring to the photo (page 75), fuse the shapes in order, starting with piece A, to the center of each 10½" x 14½" solid-colored rectangle. Make five blocks.

2. Center and pin a piece of stabilizer to the back of each block.

3. Stitch around each shape using a satin stitch and matching thread.

4. Gently remove the stabilizer.

Making the Pleated Blocks

1. With right sides together, fold each 5½" x 15½" solid-colored strip in half lengthwise. Keeping the raw edges aligned and using a ¼" seam allowance, sew along the long edge of each strip. Center the seam in the middle of each strip and press the seam open. Turn the strips right side out and press.

Make 16.

2. Mark the center of each strip with a pin. To mark the pleats, place six pins about 1" apart on each side of the center mark as shown. Fold the strip, aligning the first and third pins; then align the fourth and sixth pins to make two pleats on each side of the center mark as shown (four pleats total). Position the pleats so that the top folded edge is toward the center of the strip. Pin and press the pleats. The pleated strip should measure 2½" x 7½". Make 16 pleated strips.

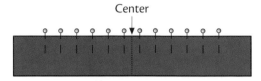

Center

Place pins 1" apart.

Fold pleats toward center.
Make 16.

3. Pin and topstitch one pleated strip from step 3 to the center of each 5½" x 7½" print rectangle as shown. Make 16 units.

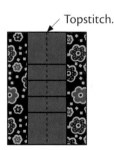

Topstitch.

Make 16.

4. Sew four units from step 4 together to make a 10½" x 14½" block. Make four.

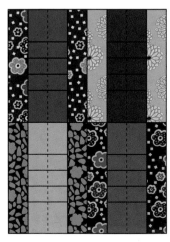

Make 4.

Assembling the Quilt

1. Refer to the assembly diagram to arrange the blocks in four rows of three blocks each, alternating the appliqué blocks and pieced blocks in each row and from row to row.

2. Stitch the blocks in each row together; press the seam allowances toward the appliqué blocks. Stitch the rows together; press the seams in one direction.

3. Layer the quilt top with the batting and backing; baste the layers together.

4. Quilt as desired. I machine quilted around each appliqué shape and then quilted the background with meandering lines, loops, and swirls, avoiding the pleated strips. Referring to "Binding" (page 15), bind the quilt using the 2½-wide brown strips.

Assembly diagram

bohemian flourish patterns

Patterns do not include seam allowances
and are reversed for fusible appliqué.

A
Cut 5.

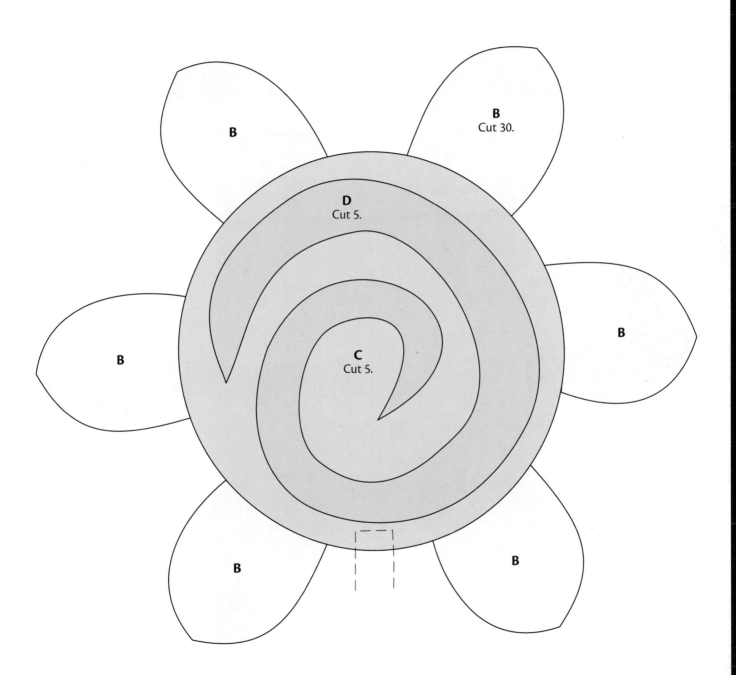

B

B
Cut 30.

D
Cut 5.

B

B

C
Cut 5.

B

B

crazy for you

Superbright and supercute, this is a quick project that's lots of fun. Use your favorite cheerful fabrics and don't be afraid to mix different colors! Let these fun circles and daisies brighten up your day. The colors pop and the flowers are full of whimsy.

Pieced and quilted by Linda Lum DeBono

Finished size: 30½" x 40½"

Materials

Yardages are based on 42"-wide fabrics. Fat quarters measure 18" x 21".

18 fat quarters **or** 18 scraps, each at least 11" x 11", of assorted lime green, turquoise, yellow, orange, royal blue, red, purple, and hot pink fabrics for appliqué-block backgrounds and flower appliqués

⅜ yard of black-and-white print for binding

1⅜ yards of fabric for backing

35" x 45" piece of batting

3 yards of fusible web

1¾ yards of stabilizer

Cutting

Measurements include ¼" seam allowances.

From the assorted fat quarters or scraps, cut a *total* of:
12 squares, 10½" x 10½"

From the black-and-white print, cut:
4 strips, 2½" x 42"

From the stabilizer, cut:
12 squares, 10½" x 10½"

Appliquéing the Blocks

1. Referring to "Fusible Appliqué" (page 14) and using the patterns (pages 80 and 81), prepare the circle and flower shapes. Referring to the photo at left and using the assorted fabrics, cut out each shape.

2. Fold each 10½" assorted square in half in both directions and lightly crease to find the center. Fuse a circle in the center of each square. Then fuse a daisy flower and flower center in the middle of each circle. Repeat to make 12 blocks.

3. Center and pin a piece of stabilizer to the back of each block.

4. Stitch around each shape using a satin stitch and matching thread.

5. Gently remove the stabilizer.

Assembling the Quilt

1. Refer to the assembly diagram to arrange the blocks in four rows of three blocks each.

2. Stitch the blocks in each row together; press the seam allowances in one direction, alternating the direction from row to row. Stitch the rows together; press the seams in one direction.

3. Layer the quilt top with the batting and backing; baste the layers together.

4. Quilt as desired. I machine quilted around each appliqué shape, and then quilted the background with meandering lines, loops, and swirls. Referring to "Binding" (page 15), bind the quilt using the 2½"-wide black-and-white strips.

Assembly diagram

crazy for you patterns

Patterns do not include seam
allowances and are reversed
for fusible appliqué.

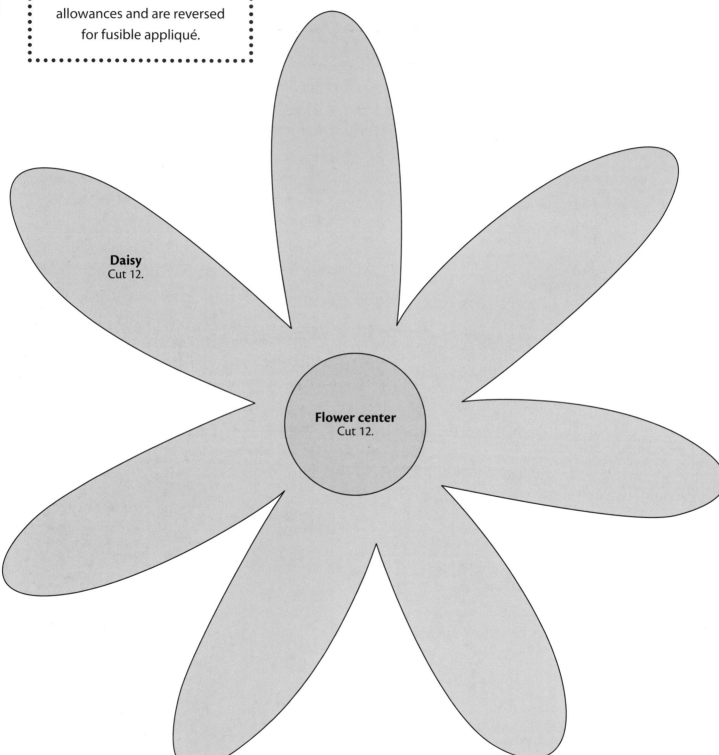

Daisy
Cut 12.

Flower center
Cut 12.

Enlarge circle pattern 125%.

Circle
Cut 12.

vintage bouquet

Give this soft and pretty quilt to a friend who loves that vintage look.

Pieced and quilted by Linda Lum DeBono
Finished size: 30½" x 50½"

Materials

Yardages are based on 42"-wide fabrics.

2 yards *total* of teal and orange fabrics for blocks and appliqué-block backgrounds

1¼ yards *total* of teal, orange, and brown fabrics for flower appliqués

⅜ yard of red print for flower appliqués

½ yard of brown fabric for binding

1¾ yards of fabric for backing

35" x 55" piece of batting

2 yards of fusible web

2¼ yards of stabilizer

Cutting

Measurements include ¼" seam allowances.

From the teal and orange fabrics, cut a *total* of:
7 squares, 11¼" x 11¼"; cut each square twice diagonally to yield 28 triangles
8 squares, 10½" x 10½"

From the brown fabric for binding, cut:
5 strips, 2½" x 42"

From the stabilizer, cut:
15 squares, 10" x 10"

Making the Pieced Blocks

Each block is made using two triangles from one of the teal or orange fabrics and two triangles from a contrasting teal or orange fabric. Arrange and sew four triangles together as shown; press. Refer to the photo at left as needed. Make seven.

Make 7.

Appliquéing the Blocks

1. Referring to "Fusible Appliqué" (page 14) and using the patterns (pages 84 and 85), prepare the flower shapes. Referring to the photo and using the red, teal, orange, and brown fabrics, cut out each shape.

2. Fold each 10½" assorted square in half in both directions and lightly crease to find the center. Fuse a large outer flower in the center of each square. Then fuse a large inner flower and flower center to the middle of each outer flower to make eight Large Flower blocks.

3. Fuse a small flower, and then a flower center, to the middle of each pieced block from "Making the Pieced Blocks" to make seven Small Flower blocks.

4. Center and pin a piece of stabilizer to the back of each block from steps 2 and 3.

5. Stitch around each shape using a satin stitch and matching thread.

6. Gently remove the stabilizer.

Assembling the Quilt

1. Refer to the assembly diagram (page 84) to arrange the blocks in five rows of three blocks each, alternating the Large Flower blocks and Small Flower blocks in each row and from row to row.

2. Stitch the blocks in each row together; press the seam allowances toward the Large Flower blocks. Stitch the rows together; press the seams in one direction.

3. Layer the quilt top with the batting and backing; baste the layers together.

4. Quilt as desired. I machine quilted around each appliqué shape, and then quilted the background with meandering lines, loops, and swirls. Referring to "Binding" (page 15), bind the quilt using the 2½"-wide brown strips.

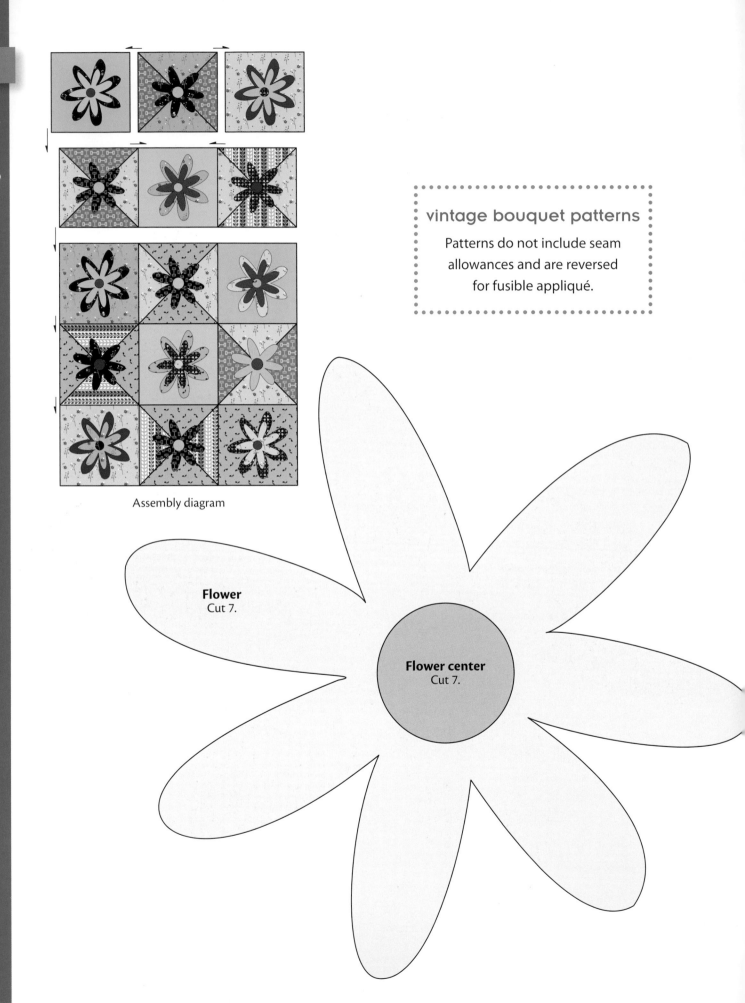

Assembly diagram

vintage bouquet patterns

Patterns do not include seam
allowances and are reversed
for fusible appliqué.

Flower
Cut 7.

Flower center
Cut 7.

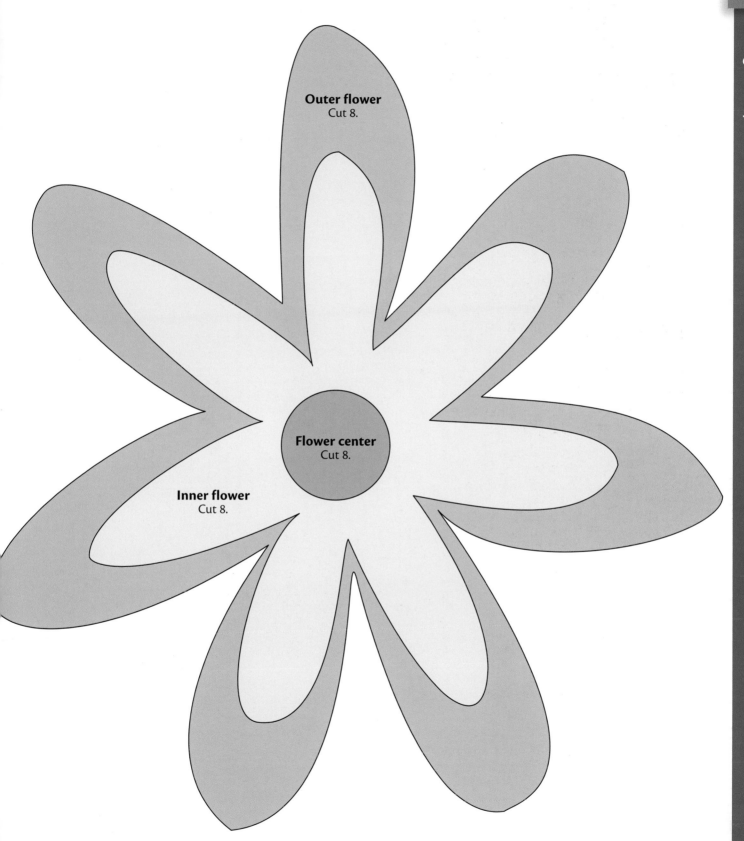

Outer flower
Cut 8.

Flower center
Cut 8.

Inner flower
Cut 8.

flowers on parade

Paisleys twirl and dance in this quilt. The blocks are reminiscent of old Byzantium floors, and the bright fabrics make the blocks come alive.

Pieced and quilted by Linda Lum DeBono

Finished size: 36½" x 36½"

Materials

Yardages are based on 42"-wide fabrics. Fat quarters measure 18" x 21".

1 fat quarter *each* of 4 or 5 blue-and-green prints for flower appliqués

⅞ yard of red tone-on-tone print for appliqué-block backgrounds

⅞ yard of red paisley print for blocks

¼ yard of green tone-on-tone print for corner squares

¼ yard of yellow print for border triangles

⅜ yard of green fabric for binding

1⅓ yards of fabric for backing

41" x 41" piece of batting

⅞ yard of fusible web

1⅛ yards of stabilizer

Cutting

Measurements include ¼" seam allowances.

From the red tone-on-tone print, cut:
5 squares, 12½" x 12½"

From the red paisley print, cut:
4 squares, 12½" x 12½"

From the green tone-on-tone print, cut:
1 rectangle, 6" x 22"

From the yellow print, cut:
1 rectangle, 6" x 28"

From the green fabric for binding, cut:
4 strips, 2½" x 42"

From the stabilizer, cut:
5 squares, 12½" x 12½"

4 squares, 6" x 6"

4 squares, 6" x 6"; cut each square once diagonally to yield 8 triangles

1 square, 6" x 6"; cut twice diagonally to yield 4 triangles

Appliquéing the Blocks

1. Referring to "Fusible Appliqué" (page 14) and using patterns A–H (page 89) and the blue-and-green fabrics, prepare and cut out the flower shapes.

2. Using the assembly diagram (page 88), fuse pieces A–F, piece G, and finally piece H to each 12½" red tone-on-tone square to make five blocks.

3. Center and pin a piece of 12½"-square stabilizer to the back of each block.

4. Stitch around each shape using a satin stitch and matching thread.

5. Gently remove the stabilizer.

Preparing the Corner Squares and Border Triangles

1. Referring to "Fusible Appliqué" (page 14), prepare the 6" x 22" green tone-on-tone rectangle with fusible web and then cut out four 5¼" squares.

2. Prepare the 6" x 28" yellow print rectangle with fusible web and cut out five 5¼" squares. Crosscut *four* of the squares once diagonally to make eight side triangles. Crosscut *one* square twice diagonally to make four corner triangles. Don't remove the paper backing from the green squares or yellow triangles until you are ready to fuse them in steps 3 and 4 in "Assembling the Quilt Top" (page 88).

Assembling the Quilt Top

1. Refer to the assembly diagram to arrange the appliqué blocks and the 12½" red paisley squares in three rows of three blocks each, alternating the appliqué blocks and paisley squares in each row and from row to row.

2. Stitch the blocks in each row together; press the seam allowances toward the paisley squares. Stitch the rows together; press the seams in one direction.

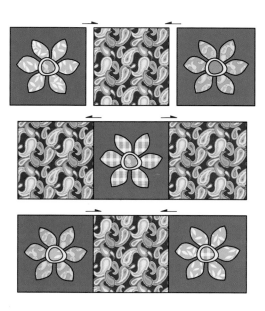

3. Using the prepared green squares, position and then fuse the squares on top of the intersecting seam lines of the quilt top as shown in the assembly diagram. Center and pin a 6" piece of stabilizer on the back of the quilt top under each green square. Stitch around each square using a satin stitch and matching thread. Gently remove the stabilizer.

4. Using the prepared yellow triangles, position and then fuse the side triangles on top of the seam lines and a corner triangle on each corner as shown in the assembly diagram. Center and pin the stabilizer triangles on the back of the quilt top under each yellow triangle. Stitch around each triangle using a satin stitch and matching thread. Gently remove the stabilizer.

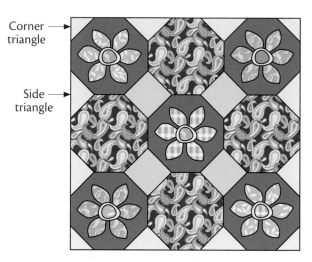

Assembly diagram

Finishing the Quilt

1. Layer the quilt top with the batting and backing; baste the layers together.

2. Quilt as desired. I machine quilted around each appliqué shape, and then quilted the background with meandering lines, loops, circles, and swirls. Referring to "Binding" (page 15), bind the quilt using the 2½"-wide green strips.

flowers on parade patterns

Patterns do not include seam allowances
and are reversed for fusible appliqué.

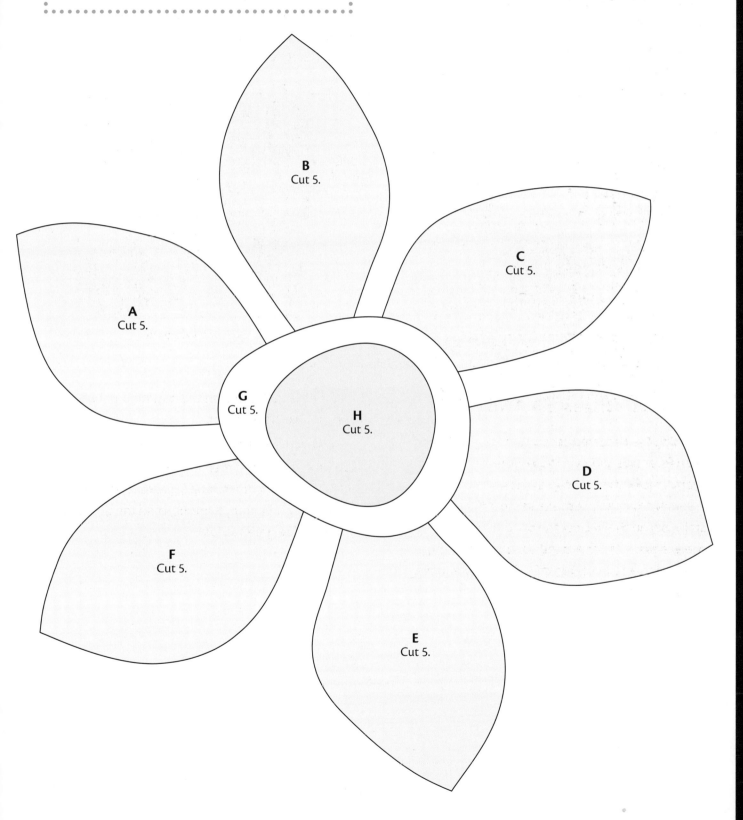

B
Cut 5.

C
Cut 5.

A
Cut 5.

G
Cut 5.

H
Cut 5.

D
Cut 5.

F
Cut 5.

E
Cut 5.

perky paisley quilt

Funky paisleys and bright flowers brighten up this fun quilt. Give this to a loved one and she will smile every time she sees it hanging in her room.

Pieced and quilted by Linda Lum DeBono

Finished size: 28¼" x 42½"

Materials

Yardages are based on 42"-wide fabrics. Fat quarters measure 18" x 21".

1⅓ yards *total* of 5 to 7 different fuchsia prints for blocks and appliqué-block backgrounds

1⅛ yards *total* of 4 different purple prints for blocks and appliqué shapes

⅜ yard *total* of 3 different lime green prints for appliqué shapes and yo-yos

Scraps of yellow print for appliqué flower centers

⅜ yard of black-and-wide stripe for binding

1½ yards of fabric for backing

33" x 46" piece of batting

1½ yards of fusible web

1¼ yards of stabilizer

4 fuchsia buttons, ¾" diameter (optional)

Cutting

Measurements include ¼" seam allowances. Template patterns for pieces F and G appear on page 94. For detailed instructions, refer to "Making Templates" (page 14).

From the fuchsia prints, cut a *total* of:

6 rectangles, 10½" x 14½"

12 pieces using template F

From the purple prints, cut a *total* of:

6 pieces using template G

6 reversed pieces using template G

From black-and-wide stripe, cut

4 strips, 2½" x 42"

From the stabilizer, cut:

6 rectangles, 10½" x 14½"

Appliquéing the Blocks

1. Referring to "Fusible Appliqué" (page 14) and using patterns A–E (page 93), prepare and cut out the appliqué shapes. Referring to the photo at left and using the fuchsia, lime green, purple, and yellow fabrics, cut out each shape.

2. Using the assembly diagram (page 92), fuse the pieces to each 10½" x 14½" fuchsia rectangle in order, starting with piece A. Make six blocks.

3. Center and pin a piece of stabilizer to the back of each block.

4. Stitch around each shape using a satin stitch and matching thread.

5. Gently remove the stabilizer.

Making the Diamond Blocks

1. Arrange and sew four fuchsia F pieces together as shown to make a large diamond shape. Offset the point at the top edge ¼" as shown; press. Make three.

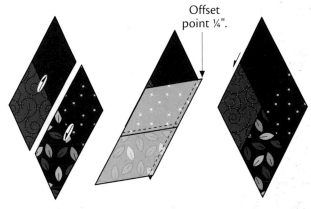

Offset point ¼".

Make 3.

2. Sew one purple G piece and one reversed G piece to opposite sides of the large diamond shape; press. Sew one purple G piece and one reversed G piece to each remaining side of the

diamond shape to complete the block; press. The block should measure 7½" x 14½", including seam allowances. Make three blocks.

Make 3.

Assembling the Quilt Top

1. Refer to the assembly diagram to arrange and sew one diamond block between two appliqué blocks to make a row. Press the seam allowances toward the appliqué blocks. Make three rows.

2. Stitch the rows together; press the seams in one direction.

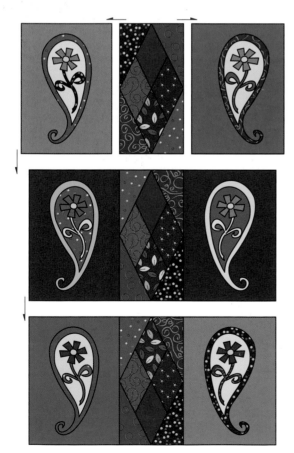

Assembly diagram

Finishing the Quilt

1. Layer the quilt top with the batting and backing; baste the layers together.

2. Quilt as desired. I machine quilted around each appliqué shape, and then quilted the background with meandering lines, loops, circles, and swirls. Referring to "Binding" (page 15), bind the quilt using the 2½"-wide black-and-white strips.

3. If desired, stitch a button to each corner of the center block.

Making the Yo-Yos

1. Refer to "Making Templates" (page 14) to trace the circle pattern (page 94) onto template plastic. Using the template, trace one circle onto the wrong side of each lime green print. Cut out the circles.

2. Thread a needle with green thread and knot the ends together. Finger-press the edges of each circle under ⅛". Sew a running stitch close along the folded edge of each circle. When you have stitched completely around the circle, pull up the thread tightly to gather the circle edge; knot the threads to secure them. The yo-yo's gathered side is the right side. Make three yo-yos.

3. Center a yo-yo in the middle of each diamond block, covering the intersecting seams. Sew a few stitches in the center of each yo-yo, stitching through all the layers to secure the yo-yo. Refer to the photo (page 90) for placement as needed.

perky paisley quilt patterns

Appliqué patterns do not include seam allowances and are reversed for fusible appliqué.

A
Cut 3 and 3 reversed.

B
Cut 3 and 3 reversed.

D
Cut 3 and 3 reversed.

E
Cut 3 and 3 reversed.

C
Cut 3 and 3 reversed.

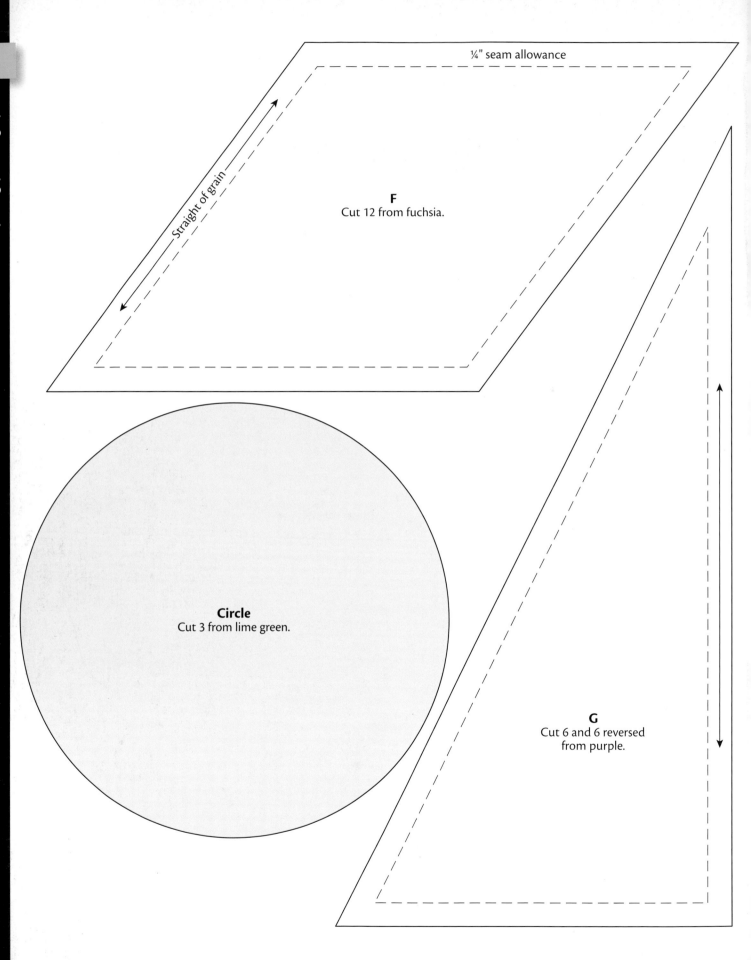

¼" seam allowance

Straight of grain

F
Cut 12 from fuchsia.

Circle
Cut 3 from lime green.

G
Cut 6 and 6 reversed
from purple.

Linda Lum DeBono has been creative her entire life. She loves knitting, quilting, scrapbooking, and paper arts. Her inspirations come from all the things around her: graphic design, architecture, greeting cards, and so on.

Before her designing life, she graduated with a bachelor of science degree from the University of Toronto in Canada, and then worked in the pharmaceutical industry for several years before moving to New Jersey with her husband.

She only started to sew when she moved to the United States and hasn't stopped since. She loves color and texture and isn't afraid to try any craft or technique once.

She lives in Clinton, New Jersey, with her supportive husband, Reno, and her two wild and crazy kids, Adam and Alex.

new and bestselling titles from

America's Best-Loved Craft & Hobby Books®
America's Best-Loved Knitting Books®

America's Best-Loved Quilt Books®

APPLIQUÉ
Adoration Quilts
Appliqué at Play
Appliqué Takes Wing
Favorite Quilts from Anka's Treasures
Mimi Dietrich's Baltimore Basics
Sunbonnet Sue and Scottie Too
Tea in the Garden

FOCUS ON WOOL
The Americana Collection—*New!*
Needle Felting
Simply Primitive

GENERAL QUILTMAKING
All Buttoned Up
Bound for Glory
Calendar Kids
Christmas with Artful Offerings—*New!*
Colorful Quilts
Comfort and Joy—*New!*
Creating Your Perfect Quilting Space
Creative Quilt Collection Volume Two
Dazzling Quilts
A Dozen Roses
Fig Tree Quilts—*New!*
Follow-the-Line Quilting Designs
Follow-the-Line Quilting Designs
    Volume Two
A Fresh Look at Seasonal Quilts
Modern Primitive Quilts
Points of View—*New!*
Positively Postcards
Posterize It!
Prairie Children and Their Quilts
Quilt Revival
Quilter's Block-a-Day Calendar
Quilting in the Country
Sensational Sashiko
Simple Traditions
Twice Quilted
Young at Heart Quilts—*New!*

LEARNING TO QUILT
Color for the Terrified Quilter
Happy Endings, Revised Edition
Let's Quilt!
Your First Quilt Book (or it should be!)

PAPER PIECING
300 Paper-Pieced Quilt Blocks
Easy Machine Paper Piecing
Paper-Pieced Mini Quilts—*New!*
Show Me How to Paper Piece
Showstopping Quilts to Foundation Piece
Spellbinding Quilts

PIECING
40 Fabulous Quick-Cut Quilts
Better by the Dozen
Big 'n Easy
Clever Quarters, Too
New Cuts for New Quilts
Over Easy
Sew One and You're Done
Snowball Quilts
Square Deal
Stack a New Deck
Sudoku Quilts
Twosey-Foursey Quilts
Wheel of Mystery Quilts

QUILTS FOR BABIES & CHILDREN
Even More Quilts for Baby
Lickety-Split Quilts for Little Ones—*New!*
The Little Box of Baby Quilts
Quilts for Baby
Sweet and Simple Baby Quilts

SCRAP QUILTS
More Nickel Quilts
Nickel Quilts
Save the Scraps
Simple Strategies for Scrap Quilts
A Treasury of Scrap Quilts

CRAFTS
101 Sparkling Necklaces—*New!*
Bag Boutique
Card Design—*New!*
Creative Embellishments
Greeting Cards Using Digital Photos
It's a Wrap
It's in the Details—*New!*
The Little Box of Beaded Bracelets
    and Earrings
The Little Box of Beaded Necklaces
    and Earrings
Miniature Punchneedle Embroidery
A Passion for Punchneedle
Punchneedle Fun—*New!*
Scrapbooking off the Page…
    and on the Wall
Sculpted Threads

KNITTING & CROCHET
365 Knitting Stitches a Year:
    Perpetual Calendar
A to Z of Knitting
Crocheted Pursenalities
First Crochet
First Knits
Fun and Funky Crochet
Handknit Style II
The Knitter's Book
    of Finishing Techniques
Knitting Circles around Socks—*New!*
Knitting with Gigi
The Little Box of Crochet for Baby
**The Little Box of
    Crocheted Throws—*New!***
The Little Box of Knitted Throws
Modern Classics
More Sensational Knitted Socks
Pursenalities
Silk Knits
Top Down Sweaters
Wrapped in Comfort